The Rangoon Sisters

COOKBOOK

The Rangoon Sisters

COOKBOOK

AMY CHUNG & EMILY CHUNG

EBURY
PRESS

for Mum and Dad

CONTENTS

INTRODUCTION

It's September 2012: we feel huge and sweaty, our generous posteriors perched on tiny plastic stools in the middle of Yangon's Bogyoke Market. Sights, smells, sounds! Mum grabs the attention of one of the staff members, yells some orders over the din, and the next thing we know, bowls of *mohinga*, noodle salad and potato curry appear along with a plate of hot, buttery flatbread. We wash it all down with watermelon juice and achingly sweet star cola. There's a feeling of comfort in our bellies. Our first Burmese meal in Burma. We are home.

We are Emily and Amy – sisters, doctors, home-cooks-come-supper-club-hosts who love to eat, feed and entertain. Our lives revolve around food, and when the two of us meet up, our proposed activities are generally framed around what and where we are going to be eating.

We were born and bred in South London, with Anglo-Burmese-Chinese heritage. The kitchen-diner was the heart of the home and we grew up watching our parents cooking, picking up skills along the way. Soon enough, we took over the cooking at Christmas and parties in our teenage years. We both ended up studying medicine and became doctors, while still maintaining a passion for cooking and entertaining. Then, in 2013, an opportunity arose for us to host a pop-up Burmese dinner in an East London pub and it took off from there; the next thing we knew, our Burmese supper club was the hottest culinary ticket in London. People seemed to really love our food, the sharing of it, the friendly atmosphere at our dinners and, of course, meeting our mum and dad, who were key players in the whole operation. A cover and double-page spread in the *Observer Food Monthly* cemented us as eminent Burmese food advocates and the cuisine was soon deemed to be the next new trend. We would argue that it's not a trend; it has always been here, and eaten widely, it just hasn't been under the spotlight. An increased awareness of and accessibility to different food cultures has piqued curiosity and spread knowledge, and with more and more people travelling to Burma in recent years, this cuisine has had more attention.

Our food isn't fancy; we don't present it in rings or do saucy drizzles or foams. The recipes in this book are all our home-cooked recipes, learned by close observation of our mum and our grandma's Burmese cooking, or created from our own recipe-testing of dishes that we've tasted over the years. We think they are accessible for all levels of home cook, and while some dishes may take a little time, they don't require any special skills. Oh, and you'll be developing a close relationship with onions… So come and have a seat at our table and make yourself at home.

A note on place names. We have adopted the former name of the former capital of Burma, Rangoon, in our brand – now known as Yangon (after the elections in 1989, many place names changed). We do not have strong feelings about whether you call the country Burma or Myanmar, but we use Burma throughout the text as this is the name we grew up using.

A note on pronunciation. Phonetic Burmese spellings vary and we have opted for what we think is the simplest. 'Ky' (for example in 'kyaw') is pronounced 'ch'.

THE FOOD OF BURMA

Like its landscape and climate, the food of Burma is hugely varied. People who haven't tried it before might feel a familiarity because of the country's location, nestled within easy reach of the wonderful influences of India, Bangladesh, Thailand and China. However, there are definitely unique qualities too, which reflect the country's long, rich and complex history.

A very condensed history begins here. Travel across Southeast Asia over the centuries led to changes in rulers and the introduction of influences from across the region, such as Buddhism from India and the Mongol invasion. After the ninth century, the Bamar people established the Pagan kingdom and this became the predominant ethnic group. In recent, more familiar history, Burma was annexed by the British Raj in the nineteenth century and became part of British India. Independence arrived in 1948, following Japanese occupation during the Second World War. Post-war, the country struggled as a result of the destruction in infrastructure that it had endured, and combined with unrest between different groups, our family made the decision to emigrate; more about that later.

We finally made our first visit to Burma with Mum, in 2012. Despite the significant changes that have occurred over time, we are always overwhelmed by the patience and kindness people have shown us when visiting Burma. On several occasions we have encountered people – effectively strangers – who would welcome us into their homes, give us tea and enjoy sharing stories, expecting nothing in return. We have been blown away by the beauty of the country, from the acres of pagoda-studded plains of Bagan, the untouched sandy beaches of Maungmagan, and the rolling hills of Shan State.

Back to food, though! A typical Burmese spread at home involves lots of small dishes for sharing:

Slow-cooked meat, poultry, seafood and vegetable curries (*hin*), which are subtly spiced but deep in flavour and seasoned oil. This layer of oil plays a key role in preserving the food, due to the absence of the widespread use of refrigeration in Burma.

Fresh, zingy salads (*a thoke*) that can be sour, salty, bitter, sweet, as spicy as you like, but also multi-textured.

Vegetable and lentil side dishes and garnishes and condiments aplenty to make your plate your own. Each mouthful becomes a 'flavour bomb'.

A plate of raw/blanched vegetables surrounding a bowl of dip, which is usually fishy or shrimpy.

Rice is a major dietary staple. It is produced extensively, is of excellent quality and is eaten at every meal. (Only small portions of meat are eaten and historically this would be due to its high cost.) Lots of vegetables, soups and rice provide the bulk of the meal, followed by fresh seasonal fruits. When people complain about the amount of oil that traditionally comes with Burmese curries, we do get a little prickly, because actually the diet is very varied and full of fruits and vegetables. It is also entirely possible to scoop the oil away, if you prefer, and still enjoy the curry underneath.

A note on fruits. Here the Alphonso is seen to be the best variety of mango, but we would argue that the ones in Burma can beat it, specifically the *Sein Ta Lone* (which translates to 'the one diamond'), though those in Burma would say if you eat too much it can make you too hot. In Burma there is a firmly held belief regarding 'hot' and 'cold' foods. For example, during winter, you should eat ginger, which is hot, and you shouldn't eat cucumber, which is cold. This idea is likely to have basis in Ayurveda, which is unsurprising due to influences from the Indian subcontinent over the centuries. The Burmese then developed it into their own style of traditional Burmese medicine. As medics, we remain sceptical about this, and yet we know that some of these concepts are followed very strictly and do in fact yield results. Illnesses may be treated by the avoidance or introduction of different types of food. Traditional Burmese medicine remains particularly important in the many remote areas that are difficult to access, and it is still popularly used alongside Western medicine.

Other excellent fruits that you can find in the markets include papaya, jackfruit, durian, watermelon and mangosteen. And this brings us to our next point, which is how great the Burmese language is and how incredibly literal a lot of translations are. A fruit called *gwei thee*, for example, translates to 'testicle fruit'. It is a sour, egg-shaped fruit, traditionally sliced and served with chilli. You will understand the reason for its name when you see it!

The geography of Burma has an influence on the cusine of different regions. The areas away from the coast, for example in the mountains, tend to utilise more meat and poultry, whereas those that can access the Ayeyarwady River in the west are blessed with delicious freshwater fish and shellfish. The coastline is extensive (nearly 2,000km in length) and produces incredible seafood. A unifying factor throughout the regions is beautiful dried shrimp, which, due to its preserved nature, means it is widely available. *Ngapi*, which is fermented and salted fish or shrimp, is a paste that to us is one of the defining smells of Burma.

You will also notice that many of our main dishes use pork or chicken. These continue to be the most popular meats in Burma. Demand for meat has been increasing since the expansion of the tourist industry and the increase in population growth, so in turn we expect livestock farming will grow too.

As the traditional Burmese saying goes,

'*A thee ma, thayet; a thar ma, wet; a ywet ma, lahpet*', which translates as: '*The best fruits are mangoes, the best meat is pork, the best leaves are lahpet.*'

Pork has always been considered a delicacy, with chicken a close second. In fact, chicken was the most expensive meat at one stage and thus was reserved for special occasions. Lamb isn't cultivated in Burma so it doesn't appear on the dinner table, although goat meat, which is known as mutton, is widely consumed around central Burma where these animals are farmed. Religious influences also determine meat choices in Burma. For example, although eating beef is not strictly forbidden in Buddhism, bovine creatures are much respected for their work in agriculture, so beef consumption is generally low. Vegetarian food can be found in Burma in abundance, though in our experience a lot of vegetable dishes do get a bit of fish sauce, dried shrimp or shrimp paste added here and there. If you prefer, these ingredients can easily be omitted in our recipes.

Burma is a diverse society, with over one hundred different ethnic groups – primarily the Bamar people, followed by Shan, Kayin, Rakhine, Kachin, Mon, Kayah and more, contributing to a diversity in regional cuisine. There is a wealth of regional specialties, often developed around what is grown and what is seasonal in the area. This is reflected in many types of dish but a good example includes noodles – sometimes served in soup, sometimes dry, sometimes with sauce. You could probably write a compendium entirely based on noodle dishes if you toured the country.

Street food is everywhere and we are very enthusiastic about it. Most common are noodle dishes as well as deep-fried delights, such as split pea fritters, lightly battered vegetables, crisp Shan tofu, Chinese dough sticks, samosas and more. All of these can be found on most street corners, ready to eat hot and fresh, and they reflect the Chinese and Indian influences that have contributed to eating habits over the years. Some of these foods can also be found in tea shops. If you have seen the opening scene of the Myanmar episode of Anthony Bourdain's *Parts Unknown*, that is the essence of the tea shop culture (in fact, that shop, *Seit Taing Kya*, was at the end of the road that Emily lived on when she was volunteering with Medical Action Myanmar in 2014). Here you can have perfect mutton puffs, Chinese-style steamed buns, naan, Indian-style *thali* or Shan noodles, all washed down with tea while you catch up with the daily newspaper and the latest gossip with your friends.

OUR HERITAGE AND FAMILY

Our recipes are family recipes, designed for sharing. Some are very typically Burmese, with a few regional variations and the occasional embellishment that family recipes acquire as they evolve. Many of them have been very successfully served at our supper clubs, while some are truly from our own personal family recipe book, which has, until now, not been shared with the world.

OUR FAMILY IN BURMA

We will start with our Anglo-Burmese grandparents, Henry and Ruby. They both had Burmese mothers and English fathers, a consequence of the social mixing that took place during colonial times. Ruby was born in Dawei, (formerly Tavoy), a small city in southeastern Burma, near the coastline and some beautiful beaches that are still relatively untouched by tourism. (At Maungmagan Beach, Emily's husband, who is English, was quite the celebrity and a few locals asked to have their photo taken with him – they hadn't met an Englishman in the flesh before.) Dawei experiences intense tropical monsoons, and when we visited in July 2014 we were wading through water-filled streets lined with wooden houses built on stilts. This was the first time we met other members of Mum's family beyond the immediate relatives, some of whom Mum had not seen for over 40 years.

Grandpa Henry was born in Yangon, but also had roots in Dawei, which is where he met Ruby. They eventually settled in Yangon, where Mum was later born and raised. Yangon (the capital city of Burma until 2005) was a busy, cosmopolitan city when Mum was growing up; it was very diverse, with Chinese, Burmese, Indians and Europeans all working and socialising with each other, and Mum's group of friends reflected that harmonious mix. Everyone bought all their produce fresh from the markets, using side cars (bicycle rickshaws) rather than cars to get around, and they would all be dressed traditionally in *longyis* (sarongs) – men in *paso* and women in *htamein*.

In the 1960s, our grandparents started planning to move. Mum was sent to boarding school in Herefordshire, England. This was understandably stressful for a then 15-year-old, as life had been good in Burma and she was about to be separated from her parents and everything she had been used to. Despite the upheaval to her life in those formative years, it is a testament to Mum that she went on to succeed, ending up working for the NHS, and doing a Masters while bringing us up. She has been a role model to us and it is she who has given us the encouragement to achieve what we have.

Our grandparents moved to Bangkok in 1967, where Grandpa was able to continue his work in shipping and while there Thai influences became a focus in their cooking and eating. They eventually moved to England, too, in 1978. Meanwhile, Mum met Dad in Worthing at a New Year's Eve party, as 1968 became 1969, where he wooed her with a bowl of instant noodles with chopped-up frankfurters.

We made our first trip to Burma in 2012, which was incredibly emotional for Mum and an eye-opening experience for us both, considering that all we knew about it was largely based on family stories and pictures in books. The country was an assault on the senses: the sights, noises, sounds, smells. There was a sea of faces, many decorated with *thanaka*, the yellow paste made from ground bark, which is used as a cosmetic and a sunscreen. We had Grandma's *thanaka* stone back home, but this was the first time we had seen it being widely used.

We visited Yangon, Mandalay, Bagan and Inle Lake, which are places often visited on the tourist trail – and for good reason. In Yangon we retraced our family's past, visiting where they used to live, although their house, sadly, was no longer there. We visited famous landmarks that left us speechless.

(clockwise from top left) Our grandma Ruby holding Mum as a baby on a beach in Sittwe; Mum and Dad on their first date in Brighton in January 1969; our grandparents Ruby and Henry

Another aspect of our travels that would continue to be a source of amusement for us was the fact that Mum was not instantly recognisable as being Burmese by the local population, which led to a lot of eavesdropping and many humorous moments. Upon arrival into Yangon we were collected from the airport by car and Mum overheard the conversation the driver was having on his mobile phone with the travel agent about where we were heading. Mum continued to speak in English to us, having slipped us a quick note with the translation: '*The older one is fat, I'm not sure she can do the stairs.*'

We just silently chuckled in the backseat. The truth was only revealed once we'd reached our destination and Mum suddenly broke into fluent Burmese, much to the driver's shock and horror. And if you were wondering, yes, the stairs were difficult – it was pitch black!

Despite this incident, we were always welcomed warmly in Burma, which was a recurring theme on our travels. There would be impromptu invitations to family homes and much-insisted gifts of fruit and *lahpet* (see page 26) as we left.

The food that we tasted as we travelled around Burma was also an experience not to be forgotten, and one we were very excited about. There were some familiar dishes that we had grown up with but there was also so much more that we hadn't encountered before. Our favourite places to eat had to be in the markets – Zawgyi in Mandalay, Bogyoke in Yangon – with their no-frills approach, just fresh, delicious *mohinga* and *thokes* (salads) eaten while sitting on plastic stools. In Zawgyi we were met with much intrigue but also great hospitality; we were given the best 'seats' in the house as everyone hurriedly surrounded us with all the electric fans they had. We were then met with endless stares as we shamelessly requested another two bowls. Honestly, portion sizes are a lot smaller there!

FAMILY AND FOOD

Food can bring so much more than just great taste and satiation, though. For example, Mum's first taste of *lahpet thoke* (pickled tea leaf salad, see page 45) on this long-awaited trip home brought tears to her eyes. It was a reminder of the food she had grown up with, but it was also a symbol of her childhood.

It's remarkable how good food can be such a powerful tool in evoking memories, many of which have been formed around the dinner table at family gatherings and special occasions. As we grew up, both Mum and Dad would cook and we enjoyed a varied cuisine – from Spag Bol to Indian-style curries and roast dinners and, of course, the food of our heritage. We would come home from school and Grandma would have prepared a plate of *buthee kyaw* (gourd fritters, see page 154) or a big pan full of *mohinga* (see pages 88 and 90). At birthdays we ate *ohn no khauk swe* (coconut chicken noodles, see page 86), which also fulfilled the Chinese tradition of eating noodles for luck and prosperity.

This exposure to a wide range of home-cooked dishes created enthusiasm in both of us to get involved in the family cooking, watching closely as Mum threw a little bit of this and a splash of that seamlessly into a pan, to make one of her many delicious curries. Grandma's pork belly curry was always a favourite, with tender, unctuous pieces of meat in a delicately spiced sauce. Both Mum and Grandma (frustratingly) never used specific amounts of ingredients in their methods, using just their innate skill and palates to create the most well-balanced flavoursome dish. Funnily enough, we soon found ourselves doing the same thing, but this book has given us the opportunity to properly document many of these recipes for everyone to enjoy.

As soon as we hit our early teens, we sisters took over cooking Christmas dinner in the family home, allowing our parents to put their feet up. For us, it was never a chore and we would scrutinise the recipe books, such as *Delia's Christmas* (cover torn and stained), Nigella's *Feast* and the seasonal issue of *Good Housekeeping* magazine, planning our menu to the finest detail before getting stuck in. The radio would be blaring out cheesy tunes, which we would undoubtedly be singing along to (did we mention we love karaoke?) while chopping and stirring, until eventually we would sit down with the rest of the family to a feast of dishes which provided a wealth of leftovers for the subsequent days.

Our parents frequently entertained family and friends, often laying on a big Chinese banquet or Burmese spread. It would never be a few simple dishes, instead there was a myriad of plates and bowls constantly coming out of the kitchen, from deep-fried wontons to samosas, curry and roasted duck, followed by at least three or four different homemade puddings, likely including a trifle, a cheesecake or a pavlova. Guests would always leave with full bellies – which is why that is something we aspire to at our supper clubs.

After we both flew the nest, Dad would make us a Chinese meal when we came home – his sweet and sour pork with black bean aubergine and lots of rice. This would be followed by at least one dessert: usually ice cream or a shop-bought pie. Food was and continues to be a celebration, inevitably with seconds, something that our husbands learnt to love whenever they came round.

It is these memories that have helped shape us and continue to inspire what we do today. We have always loved hosting and entertaining friends in our own homes and setting up our supper club became a natural extension of that.

SISTERS

We were both born and raised in South London, with five and a half years between us. We will leave it to you to guess which is the older sister (who LOVES it when asked which one is the oldest!).

Emily led the way in developing our mutual interests – a strong love for cheesy pop (Backstreet Boys being a predominant feature), celebrity gossip, travelling ... and science. We both learned to play musical instruments as children, ended up at the same secondary school and then went to medical school. Today, we continue to live within fifteen minutes of each other and it would be rare not to have asked each other 'What are you eating?' at least once a day.

Forming the supper club was something that happened naturally and it has been a success for various reasons. We know each other's likes and dislikes although, like most siblings, we also know how to rub each other up the wrong way. We both like lists too – whether that is a task list for our other halves or a to-do list before a supper club.

We both feel very grateful to be able to cook and share the food we love alongside working for the NHS. Despite medicine appearing to need quite different skills to hosting supper clubs, the truth is that these skills are in fact hugely transferable: organisation, time-keeping, team work and good communication are key. We get so much from doing both in our lives and actually, wouldn't it be wonderful if this kind of varied work life was easier to achieve for more people?

THE SUPPER CLUB

Naturally, the idea for our supper club started at a supper club. It was 2013 and we were in Ye Olde Rose and Crown pub in Walthamstow attending an American-themed 'E17 pop-up' dinner when it dawned on us that we could host our own event showcasing Burmese food. After some Dutch courage, we approached the organiser, Will Wong, now founder of the London Cookery School. We asked if we could run an event and without any hesitation he said yes (it is his – possibly blind – faith that we have to be grateful for.) We knew we could cook a decent Burmese meal, but scaling it up to serve 60 people on an evening service in a foreign kitchen was a whole different challenge.

The preparation was intense. We prepped large amounts of ingredients and scoured our cupboards for the largest pans and Tupperware we had for transferring the food to the venue. When it came to the day, adrenaline kicked in and, alongside our hard-working husbands, we pushed through to serve three courses of hot Burmese fare. When it was over, we were destroyed, with aprons splattered and legs heavy, but underneath it all there was a feeling of satisfaction and a sense that we had risen to a challenge. Our guests were great, too, and gave us some lovely feedback.

Having now well and truly caught the supper club bug, we hosted a few more events, but then Emily took a career break and spent six months volunteering in clinics in Yangon, teaching junior doctors. She then rudely came back and got pregnant, which prolonged the supper club hiatus.

Then, in 2015, the incredible chef Asma Khan was hosting a series of dinners called 'My London Supper clubs' and we volunteered to do a Burmese event, in aid of Medical Action Myanmar, for whom Emily had worked in Yangon. It reignited our passion for cooking for others and we haven't stopped since, despite work, exams and children.

There have been some notable moments for us along the way, over which we still can't help but pinch ourselves: Emily and Mum appearing on BBC Burmese, talking about Burmese food in London. Our first collaborative event with the ridiculously talented Thai-Filipino chef Sirichai Kularbwong, of Singburi.

Receiving texts one Sunday morning alerting us to our mugs being on the front cover of the *Observer* when we had been listed in the *Observer Food Monthly* 50 for 2018. It has all been a whirlwind of incredible experiences, but one of the most significant and important to us has been the wonderful people we have met and become friends with along the way. At our dinners we always try to speak to as many people as we can, and the stories they tell us continue to surprise us. It makes our day when we see our guests eating, talking, mixing and making new friends. One delightful elderly gentleman travelled several hours on the train alone and unexpectedly became the life and soul of the party, socialising with everyone and sharing his fascinating account of when he used to be a pilot in Burma. There have also been some more intriguing events, notably a couple having a row in the middle of their meal, leading to one of them leaving early while the other stayed behind and finished both of their desserts. We're pretty sure the food had nothing to do with the argument!

THE FUTURE

Writing this book has been a great opportunity for us to reflect on everything we have achieved so far and also to think about what comes next. Without a doubt we intend to continue hosting our supper clubs and introducing more people to the wonders of Burmese food, but our inner perfectionists continue to want to be challenged, as we have been many times since starting this adventure.

We have definitely changed the way we work since our very first supper club. We have learnt a great deal, and brought out new recipes, tweaking and perfecting them, streamlining our service to be the best that it can be. We have also established a great team of friends and family as our most valued helpers and, most importantly, have invested in some large hardwearing Tupperware. We continue to learn every day and we embrace new opportunities. We want to further explore the food of our heritage, eat more and cook more. And what about setting up that restaurant? Well, you never know, watch this space...

THE BURMESE STORE CUPBOARD

We have compiled a list of descriptions of the ingredients that feature in a Burmese store cupboard, as well as information on some of the fresh produce. The ingredients that are core essentials in our Burmese larder are onions, garlic, ginger, chilli, turmeric, and paprika. We expect these will already be well known to you and easily accessible, so we have not detailed these here.

Otherwise the ingredients on this list should still be largely familiar and can be sourced in the world foods aisle of the major supermarkets, with a few that may be more readily found in Asian supermarkets and online. We have compiled a list of our favourite stockists on page 214.

AGAR-AGAR

This is a setting agent made from seaweed, which makes it a great alternative to gelatine for vegetarians. It is often used in Asian desserts to create brightly coloured jellies. It can be found as powder or in long strands in a variety of different colours and is prepared by dissolving it in hot liquid. It also sets without the need for refrigeration. You can find it in most east and southeast Asian supermarkets.

BANANA STEM

This is the tender, inner part of the banana plant stem, which is sliced, and is a key ingredient of *mohinga* (see pages 88 and 90) in Burma. Its texture is reminiscent of fennel or celery when raw, but the taste (which is subtle) has no substitute. We have been told of one Indian supermarket in Gant's Hill, in east London, which has it, otherwise it is pretty impossible to get hold of in the UK. We add more shallots instead.

BASIL SEEDS

Also known as Sabja seeds. These are small black seeds which, when soaked in water, swell up to resemble miniature frogspawn within a few minutes. Yes, that might not sound too appealing, but it's quite an accurate description – see for yourself! The black centre remains but the seed develops a glutinous outer layer which provides a chewy, almost crunchy texture. They are often used in Asian desserts and drinks such as Burmese falooda. Chia seeds are a suitable substitute.

BOTTLE GOURD

Also known as calabash, dudhi or *buthee* in Burmese, this green-skinned vegetable with white flesh has a very subtle flavour. In other cuisines it is often used in curries or chutneys, but in Burma it tends to be deep-fried as fritters after being coated with a batter and can also be used to make a simple soup. Marrow can be used as a substitute.

CATFISH

This is a river fish that is so-called for its long whiskers. It is found in a number of different continents, having been farmed for many years, and is a key ingredient in *mohinga*, the traditional Burmese fish noodle soup. As catfish is not as widely available here in the UK, we have two different recipes for *mohinga* (see pages 88 and 90), one made using catfish and another using canned pilchards – a good alternative that Grandma has used for years.

CHANA DAL

Split chickpeas, lentils or pulses are a common staple in southeast Asian cooking. They are relatively cheap and have a long shelf life, which makes them a great store cupboard item. Chana dal are the inside of chickpeas, when the kernel has been removed and then split. They are ideally left to soak in water overnight before boiling to shorten the cooking time. In Burma they have a multitude of uses, from being deep-fried to make *pe kyaw* (crispy crackers, see page 148) and *paya kyaw* (chickpea fritters, see page 151) as well as being made into *dal* (see page 126). They can be used interchangeably with yellow split peas, which look very similar but are technically peas.

COCONUT

Not commonly found in Burmese dishes but still an important ingredient, particularly in *ohn no khauk swe* (coconut chicken noodles, see page 86) and desserts. Fresh coconut milk would be made from the flesh of the abundant mature brown coconut in Burma, but we find that using a good-quality tinned coconut milk such as the Thai brand Chaokoh is just as good here in England. We also use tinned coconut cream in some desserts – this is very thick coconut milk with a high solid/fat content.

We also like to use creamed coconut (which is NOT the same as coconut cream) that comes in a solid rectangular block. It is made from the dehydrated fresh pulp of a mature coconut, ground to a white creamy paste. In curries it provides a thick, creamy consistency without too much richness. Coconut milk, cream and creamed coconut can be found in most Asian and major supermarkets.

DRIED SHRIMPS

These are shrimps that have been dried and salted for preservation. They can be used whole but are also pounded into a powder to be used in salads, soups and dips. In Burma there is a wide range of grades of shrimp sold in large drums in markets, which are excellent and the best we have ever tasted. In the UK, dried shrimps are imported and sold in packets which should be stored in an airtight container in the fridge once opened. Our mum has a designated dried shrimp drawer in the fridge, which shows just how important they are in Burmese cooking. Most east and southeast Asian supermarkets stock these.

DRIED YELLOW PEAS

Also known as vatana or garden peas and usually found in Indian supermarkets. These are used in Indian cooking to make soups and dal. In Burma they are used in sprouted form, called *pe pyote* (see page 80), and are popularly served with rice, glutinous rice or naan as a simple, filling breakfast.

FERMENTED TEA LEAVES (LAHPET)

These are a significant part of Burmese food heritage and are unique to Burma, remember: '*of all the leaves, lahpet's the best*'. Young leaves are picked in the tea plantations and are then fermented, a process that involves steaming, packing into clay pots and pressing with weights. This is left to ferment over 4–6 months, leading to the development of *lahpet*'s unique taste, which we have spent several hours trying to put into words. It tastes just as you would imagine fermented tea leaves to – musty, bitter, strong. It looks like green mulch, which is hard to make sound attractive, but believe us, everyone we have introduced it to ends up loving it.

It can be served in a ceremonial tray with several divided sections (see picture opposite), with people helping themselves and mixing these together as they like. It can also be served as *lahpet thoke* (pickled tea leaf salad, see page 45) when combined with crispy beans and nuts, sesame seeds, lime, chilli, dried shrimp, fish sauce, cabbage and tomato. Traditionally *lahpet* would be served at the end of a meal, to give a little caffeine kick, much like you'd have a tea or coffee.

FISH SAUCE

Known as *ngan pyar yay*, this is a commonly used ingredient in southeast Asian cooking. It smells pungent on its own but the flavour it brings to a dish is delicious and hard to replicate. It is made by filling barrels with fish and salt, later taking off the resulting liquid which is full of umami, and which brings out the flavour in a lot of Burmese dishes. This is often our go-to ingredient when a dish needs a little something extra. Different countries have their own versions and brands; we use the Thai brands Squid or Tiparos. It is now possible to buy vegetarian fish sauce, but you could use light soy sauce as a substitute. However, we would thoroughly recommend sticking with the original, which is widely available in Asian and major supermarkets.

GARAM MASALA

A blend of Indian spices that can vary, like curry powder. It typically contains a combination of some of the following: black pepper, cloves, cardamom, coriander, cumin and nutmeg.

GRAM/BESAN (CHICKPEA) FLOUR

This is a light yellow-coloured flour that you may see called besan or chickpea flour, which is made from ground chana dal. It has a wide variety of uses in

Burmese cooking, and is another example of something brought over from India that has had a spin added to it in Burma. It is used as a thickener in *ohn no khauk swe* (coconut chicken noodles, see page 86), provides the basis of Shan tofu (see page 146) and is also toasted in a pan over the hob to be used in some of the salads, to provide a nutty quality and to bind the components together. It is gluten-free. You can find it in Asian and most major supermarkets nowadays.

GREEN PAPAYA

This is the unripe papaya before it becomes the more widely recognisable orange-fleshed fruit. It has a harder skin and the flesh is sharper in flavour and it is often used to make papaya salads (see page 59) around southeast Asia.

KAFFIR LIME LEAVES

These leaves come from the Kaffir lime plant and are popularly used in a variety of southeast Asian dishes. The leaves have a gorgeous, fresh citrus aroma which is released when they are crushed. We use them alongside our Shan tofu to create a zesty dressing (see page 42). You can get them fresh or frozen in Asian supermarkets. We purchased a plant online and have been surprised at how well it continues to grow, considering it's native to southeast Asia. So if you are feeling adventurous and green-fingered, it's worth a try.

KECAP MANIS

This is an Indonesian sweet soy sauce with a thicker, almost caramel-like consistency, which is down to the addition of palm sugar. It does taste different from the salty light soy sauce, but dark soy sauce could be used as a substitute. It makes for a great marinade ingredient and also works well in fried rice.

LEMONGRASS

A very fragrant grass that is used as a herb in southeast Asian cooking. It forms the base of Burma's national dish, *mohinga* (see pages 88 and 90), to which it adds a wonderful citrus flavour. We find that bashing the herb whole using a pestle and mortar allows the flavour to fully disperse when cooking. Fresh is best and these can now be commonly found in standard supermarkets. However, it is also possible to buy it frozen, which is an adequate alternative if buying fresh is difficult or you want to store some away for another time.

MANGO

Mangoes from Burma are simply divine. Nearly 200 different varieties are cultivated there, with the prized *Sein Ta Lone* variety considered the best. Mangoes are also used when unripe and green in a salad (see page 53), made into pickle or simply eaten as they are or with a bit of chilli and salt.

MORNING GLORY

Also known as water spinach or convolvulus, this green vegetable is commonly eaten around southeast Asia. It suits stir-frying (see page 71) as it doesn't tend to wilt down as much as your standard spinach, maintaining a bit more bite.

MUNG BEAN FLOUR

This is made from ground mung beans – green-coloured beans that are mainly grown in India and Asia. This flour is gluten-free and can be used to make noodles in both savoury and sweet dishes.

MUSTARD GREENS

These are leafy vegetables that can be used in simple stir-fries, but are commonly used pickled. In pickled form they are often used as a garnish to complement dishes such as *Shan khauk swe* (Shan noodles, see page 94). They can easily be found in pickled form in east Asian supermarkets.

NOODLES

After rice, noodles are probably the next most commonly eaten starch in Burma. A wide variety of noodles are used depending on the dish, ranging from egg noodles to rice vermicelli noodles. Noodles are also eaten cold, such as in *khauk swe thoke* (noodle salad, see page 60), or deep-fried to produce crispy noodles that are used as a garnish or snack (see page 155).

Egg noodles are probably the most well-known noodle worldwide, which are made with wheat flour and egg. We tend to use dried chow mein noodles (Lion is our preferred brand, which happens to be egg-free) in many of our dishes. The dried noodle nests are cooked in boiling water and we often mix in a little oil after draining to prevent them from sticking.

Udon noodles are a Japanese wheat-based noodle that we use as a good substitute for the *nangyi* round rice noodles used in *nangyi thoke* (rice noodles with chicken, see page 92), as they are similarly thick and round with a chewy texture. We buy them pre-cooked in sealed packets as they are quick and easy to prepare. They can also be added straight into a pan of cooked sauce or soup.

Cellophane or glass noodles are thin and made from mung beans. They are shiny and almost transparent, hence their name. They come dried and are easily cooked by soaking in boiling water. They provide an extra texture in *htamin let thoke* (rice salad, see page 135).

Rice noodles are frequently found fresh in Burma, both fermented and unfermented. In the UK, it is easier to find them in dried form, sold as rice vermicelli. They come in various sizes (referred to in the recipes) and cook very quickly by soaking in boiling water.

Flat rice noodles, such as Pad Thai or Bun, tend to require longer cooking. This is our preferred type of noodle for *khauk swe kyut kyut kyaw* (crispy fried noodles, see page 155) because they puff up nicely into lovely curly shapes, producing a light, crisp noodle.

MSG

Monosodium glutamate is a sodium salt of glutamic acid that is found naturally in foods such as tomatoes, cheese and mushrooms. It has been around for many years but has become a controversial ingredient, though there is no robust scientific evidence that it causes any physical syndrome. It is commonly used in Chinese cooking and is thought to provide enhancement and an increased umami or savoury flavour, adding extra depth to food. We leave it in your hands as to whether you want to use it.

OIL

This is a very important ingredient in Burmese cooking as it helps to impart flavour as well as historically being a means of food preservation. In Burma the main cooking oil used is peanut or groundnut, because it has a high smoke point, which makes it ideal for deep-frying, and a mild, neutral flavour. It does tend to be more expensive to buy, so we also suggest using vegetable or sunflower oil as a substitute for both stir-frying and deep-frying.

Flavoured oils are also frequently used in Burmese food. Shallot and garlic oils (see pages 200 and 202) are added to salads, bringing extra flavour, and are also used as a condiment in noodle dishes such as *shan khauk swe* (Shan noodles, see page 94) and *hsi jet khauk swe* (garlic oil noodles, see page 96).

PALM SUGAR

As the name suggests this sugar is derived from the palm plant. It is dark in colour with a treacle-like flavour. It is often sold in one large block which can be difficult to break down, unless you smash it with a pestle. Alternatively, there are packs of smaller disc-shaped pieces which can be more easily broken up. Brown sugar can be used as a substitute in recipes, though it is slightly sweeter than palm sugar.

PANDAN LEAF

This comes from the tropical plant *Pandanus amaryllifolius*, also known as screwpine, which is native to Malaysia but widely grown in southeast Asia. It gives a luminous green colour, with a delicate fragrance and taste. It is often used in desserts and sweet drinks but can also be used in savoury dishes. Fresh pandan leaves are the ideal, though you can find them frozen in Asian supermarkets. It is also possible to get pandan essence drops as an alternative, though they are not quite as intense in flavour or colour.

PEANUTS

Also known as groundnuts, and technically a legume, peanuts are eaten roasted as a snack, crushed up in salads or used to garnish noodle dishes and pressed for their oil (see OIL). They are one of Burma's major crops. We usually buy raw unsalted peanuts which we roast ourselves, either in a hot pan or in the oven. If they have their skins on and you prefer them removed, you can put the nuts into a tea towel while they're still warm and rub to remove the skins. You can buy ready roasted unsalted peanuts in some major supermarkets and raw ones in health food stores and Asian supermarkets.

POMELO

A citrus fruit similar in size and texture to grapefruit but with a much thicker rind and lighter-coloured flesh. When perfectly ripe it has a wonderful sweet flavour. It can be eaten as it comes but is also used to make pomelo salad (see page 50), often combined with dried shrimp.

RICE

Rice is always present at a Burmese meal and makes for a great accompaniment alongside curries. It is a key ingredient in one of our favourite salads, *htamin let thoke* (see page 135), where it is eaten cold alongside lots of other flavours. We tend to use long-grain rice such as Thai jasmine rice, rinsing the grains with water before cooking.

Glutinous rice is also known as sticky rice, which is what it is when cooked! It is a type of rice which is very low in amylose, which is why its grains stick together. It is used all over Asia in a variety of ways and is popular in Burmese cooking, notably in *htamanè*, a labour-intensive sticky rice dish served during festivals.

RICE FLOUR

Made from finely ground rice, this gluten-free flour has a wide range of uses across the whole of Asia, from making noodles, dosa and hoppers to being used as a thickener. Rice flour can also be used in making desserts and in baking. We use it in most of our batter recipes, as it provides a crisp and light texture.

GLUTINOUS RICE FLOUR

This is made from glutinous rice. It has a sticky texture and is gluten free. It works well in desserts, providing a lovely chewy texture such as in *pathein halawa* (see page 174).

RAU RAM LEAVES/VIETNAMESE CORIANDER

This is *Persicaria odorata*, also sometimes called Vietnamese or Cambodian mint, laksa leaves or praew leaves. It is very aromatic and the leaves have a unique fresh flavour that has been compared with mint. The leaves are popular in a variety of southeast Asian cuisine, hence the many names, in salads, stews and soups. A mix of coriander and mint can be used as a substitute.

ROSELLE LEAVES

This sour-leaved green vegetable is commonly eaten in Burma. It is often stir-fried with prawns, as in *chinbaung kyaw* (stir-fried sour leaf, see page 70), and will wilt down like spinach, but it is also used to flavour soups. Here in the UK sorrel can be used as a substitute.

SAGO/TAPIOCA PEARLS

Sago is a starch that comes from the palm tree. It is sold as dry white 'sago pearls' that expand and become more translucent when boiled in water. They are widely used in making Asian desserts and have a chewy texture and indistinct flavour, which makes them ideal for combining with other flavours, such as coconut. Tapioca pearls (derived from cassava) can be used interchangeably with sago in our recipes.

SEMOLINA FLOUR

This yellow flour produced from wheat comes in a variety of textures. We use the coarse version in our *sanwin makin* (semolina cake, see page 180), as we prefer the texture – if you can get hold of 'semolina grits', that's the ideal type. It is used worldwide in both savoury and sweet dishes.

SESAME SEEDS

Burma is one of the top producers of these seeds. We tend to use the white variety, which is more widely available and cheaper to buy. They provide a nutty taste and texture in salads, especially when toasted beforehand, but can also be used in a variety of desserts, such as our sesame praline (see page 179).

SHRIMP PASTE

Also known as *ngapi*, this is a paste made by mixing small shrimp with salt and then leaving it to ferment for a few weeks. It is widely used in southeast Asian curries and dips, and is very important in Burmese cooking. As with dried shrimp, there is a wide range of grades of paste. It is typically found in blocks or in small tubs and has a notoriously intense smell with a strong, salty taste. A little goes a long way.

SPRING ROLL PASTRY

This thin pastry is made from wheat flour. We usually keep a packet of this in the freezer for impromptu samosa-making or even a last-minute pudding emergency (rolled up Nutella cigars – so easy). We tend to use the Spring Home brand, leaving the packet out of the freezer to fully defrost for 30 minutes before use. Once the packet is opened it is best to keep the sheets of pastry moist by covering them with a damp tea towel, so they stay pliable. Once filled, this pastry gets nice and crispy when deep-fried for samosas (see page 161), and of course for spring rolls. Filo pastry can be used as a substitute.

SOY SAUCE AND SOYBEAN PASTE

Soy sauce is a Chinese condiment made from fermented soybeans and has been around for centuries, widely used in all east and southeast Asian cultures. It's very salty and adds umami. Both light and dark soy are used in Burmese cooking.

Fermented soybean paste is used as a condiment in Burma and we usually use tinned Chinese yellow soybean paste (we use the Lee Kum Kee or Amoy brands) that you can buy at east Asian supermarkets.

TAMARIND

This is a sausage-shaped (or something else we won't say) fruit with a dry outer shell that is filled with a dark brown, sticky flesh that's full of seeds. This acidic inner pulp is compressed into blocks and sold in packets at most east Asian/ Indian supermarkets and increasingly the major retailers too. When soaked in hot water, the pulp becomes pliable and the seeds can be removed, leaving a tamarind water which is used in salads and curries for its sour taste. We prefer to use tamarind pulp because it has a better flavour, but tamarind concentrate can be used as a substitute – it just requires diluting with hot water before use.

SALADS

SALADS

The concept of salad sometimes conjures up an image of leaves and wellness. For us, it is the term we use to describe Burmese *athoke*, which just means 'mixed' and while many are light dishes they can be more substantial. They are composed of a variety of ingredients, combining vegetables, sometimes noodles, condiments and garnishes, freshly mixed together in a bowl by hand and eaten immediately. There is a huge range of salads in Burma and we have included our favourites here. You get freshness and acidity with *tha yet thee thoke* (green mango salad, see page 53) or *gin thoke* (ginger salad, see page 54), whereas *samusa thoke kalar* (Indian-style samosa salad, see page 56) is more warm and filling, served with a spiced broth. *Kyet thar thoke* (spiced chicken salad, see page 46) is a perfect way to use up leftover roast chicken (or indeed any leftover roasted meat). And of course, the salad that has gone down a storm at our supper clubs – *lahpet thoke* (pickled tea leaf salad, see page 45) – pickled tea with its unique flavour profile, crunchy nuts and beans – a heavenly, caffeinated pick me up.

Salads are quick to rustle up. A fridge forage can lead to a great salad, lifted to new levels with flavoured oil, crunchy garlic or shallots and toasted gram flour (all of these you'll find in our Sauces, Dips and Garnishes chapter (see page 196) – they can be made in bulk and can become store cupboard staples!). Texture is important, combining soft, crunchy, crisp … and dressings can be spicy, sour, sweet, salty. You can adjust these to your own preferences as you go along. The Burmese salad is very flexible and hopefully the recipes in this chapter will get you inspired to invent your own creations.

Khayan jin thee thoke

TOMATO AND CRUNCHY PEANUT SALAD

Serves 4 as a side

This salad contrasts crunchy peanuts with vibrant fresh tomatoes. Use the best-quality tomatoes you can buy to get the most out of this dish. It is best made fresh on the day, and can be served as a side with one of our curries or just simply with some rice.

50g unsalted roasted peanuts

300g tomatoes, at room temperature, quartered

½ green finger chilli, deseeded (optional) and finely sliced

1 tbsp dried shrimps (optional)

1–2 raw shallots, peeled and thinly sliced

3–5 tbsp garlic oil (see page 202)

Juice of ½ lime

2 tsp fish sauce (omit to make vegetarian, then season with salt)

Small handful of coriander leaves

1 tsp gram flour, toasted (see page 203)

Crispy fried shallots (shop-bought or see page 200), to garnish

Crush the peanuts using a pestle and mortar or pulse a few times in a food processor (to the size of the nubs you get in a shop-bought crunchy peanut butter).

Place the tomatoes, chilli, crushed peanuts and remaining ingredients in a large bowl and mix. Ideally, do this with clean hands to fully combine all the ingredients. Taste and adjust the seasoning, adding more fish sauce or chilli if necessary.

Transfer to a serving dish and garnish with the crispy shallots.

Tohu thoke

SHAN (CHICKPEA) TOFU SALAD

Serves 4 as a main, 6 as a side

1 batch of Shan tofu (see page 146), sliced into 4cm-long pieces (finger-sized pieces also work well)

2 tbsp gram flour, toasted (see page 203)

For the Kaffir lime and soy dressing

2 tbsp soy sauce

8 fresh Kaffir lime leaves, stems removed, very thinly sliced

2 tbsp shallot oil (see page 200)

1–2 tsp chilli flakes

5–6 tbsp crispy fried shallots (shop-bought or see page 200), to garnish

OR

For the tamarind garlic dressing

4 tbsp tamarind water (see page 204)

3 tbsp garlic oil

Handful of chopped coriander leaves

1 tsp chilli flakes, plus extra to taste

2 tsp fish sauce

3 tbsp crispy fried garlic (see page 202), to garnish

In Burma, we have eaten this salad with various different combinations of dressings and garnishes. Here the two dressings are quite different but equally delicious; both are fresh, light and set off by the contrasting texture of their crispy garnishes.

Place the sliced tofu in a large bowl. Next, mix the salad. We do this by pouring the prepared dressing ingredients and toasted gram flour over the tofu, then mixing everything together with two spoons or your hands.

Serve immediately.

Lahpet thoke

PICKLED TEA LEAF SALAD

Serves 4 as a side

One unique ingredient to Burma is *lahpet* – pickled tea leaves. They have a slight astringent quality, which is brought alive by being mixed into a salad along with crunchy fried beans and nuts, crispy garlic, acidic lime and sweet, tangy tomatoes. The great thing is you can now buy *lahpet* online (see page 215), so you won't have to ask your friends and relatives to bring it back for you from Burma in their suitcases.

75–100g white cabbage, very thinly sliced
2 medium tomatoes, very thinly sliced
1 tbsp dried shrimps (optional)
75g lahpet (see stockists, page 215)
100g crunchy bean mix (see page 156)
3 tbsp garlic oil (see page 202)
1 tbsp fish sauce (or vegan fish sauce)
Juice of 1 lime
½ tsp monosodium glutamate (optional; we know there are haters, so we leave it up to you)
1–2 green finger chillies, sliced

Put the sliced cabbage and tomatoes into a large mixing bowl.

If you are including them, pound the dried shrimps using a pestle and mortar or pulse in a food processor until they resemble a powder.

Add the remaining ingredients except the chillies and mix thoroughly. Taste and adjust the seasoning with fish sauce or more lime if needed. Add the chilli as per your desired spice tolerance level (we would use two), mix again and serve immediately.

Cook's notes

We use lahpet leaves whole but you can pound or chop them to a more paste-like consistency if you prefer. You could also mix in some raw chopped-up garlic and/or ginger, if you like.

Kyet thar thoke

SPICED CHICKEN SALAD

Serves 4 as a main

Here we cook the chicken fresh for this salad, but you could always make this using leftover roast chicken; we have also made this for several supper clubs using the fried chicken on page 167. We would recommend keeping the skin on the thighs when roasting them, because it keeps the flesh moist and the cooked chicken skin adds a wonderful crispy texture to the salad.

4 chicken thighs, skin on
½ tsp turmeric powder
½ tsp paprika
½ tsp chilli powder
Pinch of salt
½ medium-sized white cabbage
    (about 450g), finely sliced
Juice of 3 limes
5 tbsp garlic oil (see page 202)
5 tsp fish sauce
1 tsp chilli flakes
4 shallots, finely sliced
4 tsp gram flour, toasted
    (see page 203)

To serve
Coriander leaves
Chilli flakes
Crispy fried shallots (shop-bought
    or see page 200)

Preheat the oven to 200° C/400° F/gas mark 6.

Coat the chicken thighs with the spices and the salt and place on a baking tray in the oven. Roast for 35 minutes (check they are cooked by piercing them – the juices should run clear), then set aside to cool.

Roughly shred the chicken with a fork and knife and place in a large bowl.

Add the rest of the ingredients, except for the garnishes, and mix well.

When ready to serve, divide the salad among four plates, then garnish each with the coriander, a sprinkle of chilli flakes and a teaspoon of fried shallots. Serve immediately.

Khayan thee thoke

SMOKED AUBERGINE SALAD

Serves 4 as a side

This is one of our supper club favourites – smoky aubergines combined with tart lime, crispy garlic and roasted peanuts. Very simple, full of strong flavours and easy to make in advance, you can store the smoked aubergines in a container in the fridge until needed, then take them out and allow them to come to room temperature. Add the garnishes just prior to serving. *(Recipe pictured on page 38.)*

2 medium aubergines
Juice of 1 lime
1 tsp fish sauce (optional)
2–3 tbsp garlic oil (see page 202)
Handful of roasted unsalted peanuts
1 shallot, peeled and finely sliced

Begin by smoking the aubergines. We line our gas hob with foil, put the extractor fan on and open the windows, then put the gas on high and stick the aubergines directly on the hob burners. Using tongs, turn the aubergines every few minutes, until they are soft and burned (this will take 10–12 minutes). If you don't have a gas hob, you could do this under a hot grill but it will take a little longer. Leave the smoked aubergines on a plate to cool.

Once cool enough to handle, carefully peel off and discard the blackened skin. Halve the aubergines lengthwise, then slice into thin pieces along the width. Set aside on a plate.

Add half the lime juice to the aubergine, reserving the remaining half to add to taste after mixing if it needs more tartness. Pour over the fish sauce, then spoon over the garlic oil and scatter with roasted peanuts and sliced shallot. Mix everything together, then serve immediately.

Shauk thee thoke

POMELO SALAD

Serves 6 as a side

In Burma you would use citron to make this, but pomelo works perfectly in this sweet, salty and, let's be honest, funky salad. Sometimes a pomelo can be hit and miss, and you won't know until you crack into that thick skin, so we try to get them early in the season (January) to be sure they've not been lingering at the grocers and drying out.

½ pomelo, peeled and segments removed from membranes

2 shallots, peeled, halved and thinly sliced

1 tbsp dried shrimps

1 tsp shrimp paste

2 tbsp gram flour, toasted (see page 203)

3 tbsp shallot oil (see page 200)

2 tsp dried chilli flakes

4 tbsp crispy fried shallots (shop-bought or see page 200)

Break up the pomelo segments into bite-sized pieces and a few flakes here and there and place in a large bowl. Add the shallots.

Pound the dried shrimps to a powder using a pestle and mortar (or blitz in a food processor). Set aside.

Now for the stinky bit (you might want to close the kitchen door and open the window). Toast the shrimp paste in a frying pan for 2 minutes then scrape into a small bowl or mug. Add a teaspoon of water to this and mix.

Pour the shrimp paste-y water, dried shrimp powder, toasted gram flour, shallot oil and chilli flakes into the pomelo bowl. Mix well with your hands or a couple of spoons to coat all the fruit with the flavourings. Taste to check if you need to add more chilli.

Add the fried shallots and serve after giving the salad one final mix.

Tha yet thee thoke

GREEN MANGO SALAD

Serves 6–8 as a side

The green unripe mango is crisper and sharper in flavour than the more well-known sweet, ripe fruit, and it makes a unique, tasty salad. Just like green papaya, green mango can be found in most Asian supermarkets, but if you can't find it, a tart Bramley apple would also work well.

1 green mango (about 500g), peeled and coarsely grated

1 bird's eye red chilli, finely sliced (seeds in if you like it spicy), plus 1, sliced, to garnish

4 tbsp shallot oil (see page 200)

2 tsp fish sauce

3 tsp palm sugar

6 tbsp crispy fried shallots (shop-bought or see page 200), plus 1 tbsp to garnish

2 large handfuls of roasted, unsalted peanuts, coarsely ground

Place the grated mango into a large mixing bowl. Add the rest of the ingredients and mix well.

Tip the salad onto a serving plate and garnish with the chilli and the extra spoon of fried shallots. Serve immediately.

Gin thoke

GINGER SALAD

Serves 4 as a side

75–100g white cabbage, very thinly
    sliced
75g pickled white ginger/sushi ginger,
    drained (keep 2 tbsp of the pickling
    juice)
1 medium tomato (optional), thinly
    sliced
100g crunchy bean mix (see page 156)
2 tbsp garlic oil (see page 202)
½ tsp salt
½ lime

This is a very refreshing and sharp salad that works well with some of the oilier curries. You can pickle your own ginger but personally we find it's not always easy to find young ginger root, and pre-prepared sushi ginger does the trick just as well!

Place the sliced cabbage, drained ginger and tomato in a large bowl. Add the reserved pickling juice, crunchy bean mix, garlic oil and salt and mix thoroughly.

Squeeze over the juice from your lime half and serve immediately.

Samusa thoke kalar

**INDIAN-STYLE
SAMOSA SALAD**

Serves 2

Somewhere between a soup and a salad, here we have Indian flavours in a broth that's slightly thickened with gram flour and served topped with samosas, fresh mint and slices of lime. The contrast of smooth hot soup with crunchy but soft samosas is a winner and a very popular choice in Burmese tea shops. You could also add some *paya kyaw* (chickpea fritters, see page 151).

2 garlic cloves, peeled
½ thumb-sized piece of ginger, peeled
2 tbsp oil (vegetable, sunflower or
    peanut)
½ tsp mustard seeds
1 medium onion, chopped
½ tsp cumin powder
½ tsp paprika
½ tsp chilli powder
½ tsp turmeric powder
Salt, to taste
1 heaped tbsp gram flour
400ml vegetable stock
2 tbsp tamarind water (see page 204),
    plus extra to taste

To serve
2–3 warmed samosas, cut into
    bite-sized chunks (see page 161)
Small handful of fresh mint leaves
Small handful of thinly sliced white
    cabbage
1 lime, cut into wedges

Pound the garlic and ginger to a paste using a pestle and mortar or blitz in a food processor.

Heat the oil in a saucepan, then add the mustard seeds and stir. Once they start popping, add the chopped onion and fry until soft, for about 5 minutes.

Add the ginger and garlic paste and stir for 1 minute, then add the rest of the spices and a pinch of salt. Mix well. Stir in the gram flour, then add the vegetable stock, bit by bit, stirring continuously. It will thicken after a few minutes.

Add another 100ml of water and bring to a gentle simmer, covered, for about 15 minutes. Finally, stir in the tamarind water and taste, then adjust the seasoning with salt if necessary and, depending on how sour you like things, you could add more tamarind water.

Divide the soup among two wide, shallow bowls and top with your crunchy samosas. Garnish with mint, cabbage and serve with some lime wedges alongside. Enjoy.

Samusa thoke bamar

BURMESE-STYLE SAMOSA SALAD

Serves 2

This is a 'dry' samosa salad, which is packed full of texture and flavour. Even though this should be eaten at room temperature we would recommend heating the samosas a little beforehand so that they can crisp up. You can use *paya kyaw* (chickpea fritters, see page 151) instead of samosas, if you prefer.

50ml hot water

25g tamarind pulp

¼ small white cabbage (roughly 175g), finely sliced

1 medium tomato, sliced

1 shallot, peeled and finely sliced

1 tsp chilli flakes

4 tbsp garlic oil (see page 202)

1 tbsp gram flour, toasted (see page 203)

Juice of ½ lime

Small handful of coriander, chopped, plus extra to garnish

4 samosas (see page 161)

1 tbsp crispy fried shallots (shop-bought or see page 200)

Prepare the tamarind by adding the hot water to the pulp in a bowl and leave for a few minutes. Use a fork to further break up the pulp, then strain through a sieve, discarding any stones, so that you are left with the tamarind water. Allow to cool.

Place the rest of the salad ingredients, except the samosas and fried shallots, in a large mixing bowl with the tamarind water. Mix well.

Just before serving, slice the samosas into bite-sized chunks and mix with the salad along with the crispy shallots.

Assemble the salad on a serving plate and garnish with extra coriander. Serve immediately before the samosas and shallots have a chance to go soggy.

Thin baw thee thoke

PAPAYA SALAD

Serves 6–8 as a side

Many Asian countries have their own version of papaya salad; the Burmese recipe has a familiar spicy and sour kick, and this is our take on it. It is important to note that green papaya is the unripe version of the more commonly encountered orange papaya, which is stocked in most Asian supermarkets. The flesh is firmer so it can be shredded and it has a much lighter colour and milder taste that lends itself well to the addition of other flavours and textures.

50g tamarind pulp

100ml boiling water

2 tbsp dried shrimps

1 green papaya (about 500g), peeled and coarsely grated

2 bird's eye red chillis, finely chopped

4 tbsp garlic oil (see page 202)

Juice of 1 lime

2 tbsp fish sauce

2 tbsp gram flour, toasted (see page 203)

Large handful of coriander, roughly chopped, plus extra to serve

4 tbsp crispy fried garlic (see page 202), plus 1 tbsp extra to serve

Prepare the tamarind by adding the boiling water to the pulp in a bowl and leave for a few minutes. Use a fork to further break up the pulp, then strain the pulp through a sieve, discarding any stones, so that you are left with the tamarind water. Leave to cool.

Pound the dried shrimps using a pestle and mortar or use a food processor to create a shrimp powder.

Place the grated papaya into a large mixing bowl, then add the tamarind water, shrimp powder and the rest of the ingredients and mix well.

Tip the salad out onto a serving plate, then garnish with the coriander and fried garlic. Serve immediately.

Khauk swe thoke

NOODLE SALAD

Serves 4

This salad is best eaten at room temperature and mixed together with your hands just before serving. The onion fritters are optional but they do add a nice texture. You could add fried shallots instead if you want to save some time. This can easily be made vegetarian by omitting the shrimp and fish sauce. *(Recipe pictured overleaf.)*

25g tamarind pulp

50ml boiling water

2 tbsp dried shrimps

250g dried chow mein or egg noodles, cooked and cooled

¼ small white cabbage (roughly 175g), finely sliced

6 tbsp garlic oil (see page 202), plus extra to serve

3 tbsp fish sauce

1 tbsp gram flour, toasted (see page 203)

1 tsp chilli flakes, plus extra to serve

8–10 onion fritters (see page 150), to serve (optional)

Prepare the tamarind by adding the boiling water to the tamarind pulp in a heatproof bowl and leave for a few minutes. Use a fork to further break up the pulp, then strain it through a sieve, discarding any stones, so that you are left with the tamarind water. Leave to cool.

Pound the dried shrimps to form a powder using a pestle and mortar or a food processor.

Place all the remaining salad ingredients except the chilli flakes and fritters in a large bowl and mix well. Transfer to a serving plate and garnish with the chilli flakes and onion fritters, if using. Serve immediately with the extra garlic oil and chilli flakes on the side.

Mone lah u nee thoke

CRUNCHY CARROT SALAD

Serves 4 as a side

1 heaped tbsp sesame seeds
1 tbsp dried shrimps
300g carrots, coarsely grated
2 tbsp fish sauce
Juice of 2 limes
Handful of coriander, finely chopped

This crunchy salad has toasted notes that makes it a great accompaniment to rice and curries, or even as a change from your usual creamy coleslaw for a barbecue. If your carrots are quite juicy, just leave them in a colander for a few minutes once you have shredded them to drain away the excess water. (*Recipe pictured overleaf.*)

Toast the sesame seeds in a dry frying pan until they are lightly golden, then tip them out onto a plate and set aside. Keep a close eye on the seeds as they toast, as they burn easily.

Pound the dried shrimps to form a powder using a pestle and mortar or food processor.

Place the grated carrots in a large bowl, then add the rest of the ingredients and mix well. Serve immediately.

STIR-FRIES AND QUICK COOKS

ဟင်းရှက်ကြော်

STIR-FRIES AND QUICK COOKS

This is a chapter of stir-fried and fried dishes which do not require much preparation or cooking in advance. Stir-frying is a technique that originated in Chinese cooking and is now used globally, in which a small amount of oil is heated until super hot and the food is cooked rapidly and served immediately. As a result, vegetables like the *gazun ywet kyaw* (stir-fried morning glory, see page 71) tend to retain their colour and crunch. One of our strong childhood memories is of Mum stir-frying veg with some extremely pungent chillies, leading to a toxic chilli fog filling the kitchen and causing us to have a coughing fit every time we came downstairs.

After our dad got an allotment, we strongly encouraged him to grow sorrel so that we could readily make *chinbaung kyaw* (stir-fried sour leaf, see page 70), which has a wonderful citrus flavour that is well complemented by the addition of shrimp paste.

In addition to the vegetable dishes, our *ngar kyaw* (see page 78) takes a simple fish to new depths when fried whole and served alongside a punchy dressing. *Kyet thar athe* (see page 81) also transforms a very cheap, underappreciated ingredient like chicken livers into a spicy, warming, easy mid-week meal.

We have mainly included recipes with ingredients that are generally easy to get hold of in the West, to give you the freedom to make as many of these as possible. Feel free to substitute the different vegetables as you like; for example, you could use Tenderstem broccoli instead of morning glory, or vary the type of green beans (using French, mangetout, sugar snaps) used in *pe thee kyaw* (see page 76).

Kachin ame thar

KACHIN POUNDED BEEF

Serves 4

We discovered this fragrant and fiery dish when visiting Burma. Kachin is the northernmost state in Burma, which we would love to visit and, if this dish is anything to go by, explore the food there. The rau ram leaves add an incredibly aromatic flavour, but they are not easy to find even in Asian supermarkets, so we bought a plant on eBay and it's flourishing on our sunny windowsill. Alternatively, just use standard coriander and this will still be delicious. Be warned – the pounding to make the paste requires a strong arm and ideally a large mortar!

Oil (vegetable, sunflower or peanut), for frying
500g stewing beef, diced into 1.5cm cubes
2 thumb-sized pieces of ginger, peeled
8 garlic cloves, peeled
4–5 red bird's eye chillies, plus extra (this is meant to be spicy), thinly sliced
Handful of mint leaves, finely chopped
Handful of rau ram/Vietnamese coriander leaves, finely chopped
Juice of 2 limes
1 tbsp fish sauce
5 tbsp peanut oil
Salt

Add a glug of oil to a casserole dish set over a medium heat, then once hot, add the diced beef and cook until browned. Pour enough water into the pan to just cover the beef, bring to a simmer and cook, covered, for 40 minutes.

Remove the beef cubes with a slotted spoon and transfer to a clean dish, then discard the cooking liquid. In a wok or frying pan, pour in oil to a 4cm depth over a medium-high heat. Once hot, add the beef pieces and fry, stirring, for 3–4 minutes. Place the beef onto a plate lined with kitchen paper and set aside to cool for 10 minutes.

Get your pestle and mortar ready. Unless you are lucky enough to have a huge mortar, you will need to do this in two halves. Firstly, add the ginger, garlic cloves, sliced chillies and a generous pinch of salt. Pound to a coarse paste, then add the beef chunks and continue to pound (hopefully you have a friend who can share the workload). The meat chunks will become stringy and soft, losing their cube shape. You can use a spoon to mix everything in the mortar before pounding again.

Scoop out the mortar contents onto a plate. Add the chopped herbs, lime juice, fish sauce and peanut oil and mix well. If it seems too dry you can add a bit more oil. Serve at room temperature, with some additional chillies on the side for those who can take it.

Cook's notes
It's nice to serve this on a banana leaf!

Chinbaung kyaw

STIR-FRIED SOUR LEAF

Serves 4 as a side

Chinbaung are roselle leaves, abundant in markets in Burma but a little hard to find in the UK. However, sorrel is a very reasonable substitute which is really easy to grow and you could plant some in a pot in your outside space. This dish is quick and incredibly tasty, combining spicy with sour. You could make a vegetarian version without the shrimp elements. *(Recipe pictured on page 66.)*

3 tbsp oil (vegetable, sunflower or peanut)

1 medium onion, chopped

3 garlic cloves, peeled and thinly sliced

1 tsp shrimp paste (leave out for vegetarians)

1 tsp turmeric powder

2–3 whole green finger chillies (or 1–2 tsp chilli powder)

200g prawns, diced into pea-sized pieces (optional)

200g sorrel leaves, washed thoroughly

1 tbsp fish sauce (vegan fish sauce for vegetarians)

1 tsp sugar

Heat the oil in a large wok or frying pan over a medium-high heat. Fry the onion for 5 minutes until soft and beginning to colour, stirring occasionally to prevent sticking or burning, then add the garlic slices and stir everything around for 1 minute.

Add the shrimp paste, turmeric and chillies and stir well. Then fry off the prawns in the spicy mix for 1 minute. Turn the heat down to low-medium and add the sorrel leaves. They will wilt down like spinach and go slightly brown (entirely normal!), so stir them around to get the uncooked leaves softened. Season with the fish sauce and add the sugar.

Serve immediately with your other dishes.

Storage notes
This can be stored in a container in the fridge for up to 4 days.

Gazun ywet kyaw

STIR-FRIED MORNING GLORY

Serves 4 as a side

This vegetable has many names: morning glory, water spinach or convolvulus. It grows throughout southeast Asia and adorns many dining tables as a quick-to-cook and tasty vegetable side dish. Most southeast Asian supermarkets stock this nowadays. You could skip the shrimp paste here and replace it with a splash of soy sauce to make it veggie friendly, if you like. *(Recipe pictured overleaf.)*

2 tbsp oil (vegetable, sunflower
   or peanut)
3 garlic cloves, peeled and sliced
300g morning glory/water spinach,
   cut into 6cm lengths
1–2 red bird's eye chillies (seeds
   removed, depending on your
   tolerance), sliced
1 tsp shrimp paste (or replace with soy
   sauce for vegetarians)

Things happen hot and fast with this dish, so have all the ingredients prepared before you start cooking.

Heat the oil in a wok over a high heat – you want it smoking. Add the garlic and stir for 20 seconds, before adding the morning glory and chilli.

Keep stirring the contents of the pan, then add the shrimp paste, mixing well. Add a splash of water and stir-fry for about a minute – it should cook very swiftly if the oil and pan are hot hot hot.

Serve immediately.

Dhaw but pe hin

BUTTER BEAN STEW

Serves 3–4 as a side

3 tbsp oil (vegetable, sunflower
 or peanut)
1 medium onion, thinly sliced
250g cooked butter beans
 (tinned is fine)
1 tsp turmeric powder
½ tsp medium chilli powder
½ tsp salt

A common side dish in Burma and ridiculously easy to whip up, this makes a great back-up if you have tins of beans at home. Make this as spicy as you like.

Heat the oil in a frying pan or wok over a medium-high heat. Once you can feel the heat coming off the pan, add the onion and fry for 5–10 minutes until crispy and brown, stirring frequently.

Add the beans, turmeric, chilli powder and salt and stir well. Allow to warm through, then serve.

Pe thee kyaw

FRIED GREEN BEANS

Serves 4 as a side

Another quick-to-cook vegetable side dish which will augment any dinner spread. If you don't have dried shrimps it'll still be tasty, but they do add a little umami and saltiness, which works a treat.

1 tbsp oil (vegetable, sunflower or peanut)
1 tbsp dried shrimps (optional)
1 garlic clove, peeled and finely chopped
300g trimmed green beans
1 tsp soy sauce

Heat the oil in a frying pan, then add the dried shrimps, if using, and garlic and stir-fry for a minute or 2 until aromatic.

Add the green beans to the pan and stir-fry for 3 minutes. Add the soy sauce and a splash of water, then allow to cook for a further couple of minutes (test a bean to ensure it's tender).

Serve immediately.

Ngar kyaw

FRIED WHOLE FISH WITH FRAGRANT DRESSING

Serves 2 generously

For the dressing
6 garlic cloves, peeled
Handful of coriander (stems can be included)
1–2 red bird's eye chillies (depending on your spice tolerance, you can remove the seeds)
Juice of 2 limes
2 tbsp fish sauce

2 whole sea bream, gutted, cleaned and scaled (350–400g each)
Turmeric powder
Salt and pepper
Oil (vegetable, sunflower or peanut), for frying

When Emily was living in Yangon in 2014, there was a stall at the end of the road selling fried, fresh fish served with this tart, spicy and zingy dressing. So, of course, we had to recreate it. We would recommend ventilating the room well when cooking this dish!

First, prepare the dressing: put all the ingredients in a food processor and blitz together for 20–30 seconds, or chop the garlic and coriander very finely, thinly slice the red chillies and put them into a bowl with the other ingredients and stir.

Pat the fish dry with some kitchen paper. With a sharp knife, make slashes in the flesh to the ribcage on both sides of the fish, about 1.5cm apart. Rub a layer of turmeric into the slashes and season with salt and pepper on both sides and in the cavity.

Line a plate with a few sheets of kitchen paper. Heat enough oil in a large wok or frying pan to a depth of about 4cm. When the oil is beginning to smoke (at about 180° C), gently submerge one of the bream into the oil – it will sizzle furiously. The tail may poke out of the oil, but that's OK. Keep a close eye on the pan and fry for about 5 minutes.

Carefully lift out the fish, drain the excess oil and place the fish on the kitchen paper. Repeat the process for the second fish (or you can fry both in the same pan if they fit!).

Place the fish on a clean serving platter and pour over the dressing, getting it into the slashes. Serve immediately – this is great with plain rice and steamed vegetables.

Pe pyote

BURMESE SPROUTED PEAS

Serves 4 (with rice)

These versatile peas are frequently seen at breakfast, served with rice, or atop a *nanpyar* (Burmese naan) or stuffed in a *palata* (flatbread, see page 164). Please don't be deterred by the rather unglamorous translation; they are a great source of protein and fibre and make an excellent start to the day! The only drawback is that they take time to prepare; the dried yellow peas, which you can find in Indian supermarkets, need to be soaked and kept damp for 36–48 hours, to give them time to sprout prior to cooking. However, they can be stored in the fridge for a few days, so it's worth doing a bulk batch to have some ready to be used in a variety of ways during the week.

150g dried yellow peas (sometimes called 'Vatana' peas)
½ tsp bicarbonate of soda
1 tsp salt
2 tbsp oil (vegetable, sunflower or peanut)
1 medium onion, diced
1 tsp turmeric powder

Begin the sprouting process 3 days before you need the peas. Leave the peas to soak in a bowl with plenty of cold water overnight. In the morning, they should have increased in size. Drain through a colander and rinse thoroughly with cold water.

Dampen a clean tea towel or muslin and use this to line a large bowl. Place the peas in the cloth, then bring the ends together so the peas are completely covered and in contact with the material.

Over the next 2 days, check the peas at least 3 times a day, to ensure the tea towel is still damp and move them around a bit so that they are still getting contact with moisture. You will notice them begin to sprout; this will depend in part on the temperature – during winter in London it tends to take about 48 hours.

Once they've sprouted, rinse the peas in a colander. Place the drained peas in a saucepan with the bicarb, ½ teaspoon of salt and enough water to fully cover the peas and bring to the boil. Once boiling, lower the heat to a simmer, then cook for 50–60 minutes – they will become tender and easily squashable with a fork when ready. Check one; if it's still on the hard side, keep simmering. If the pan is starting to boil dry, top up with more water. Once the peas are tender, drain and rinse again. They can now be eaten as they are, stored in the fridge for eating later, or sautéed.

To sauté, heat the oil in a large frying pan or wok and fry the diced onion for 5 minutes or so until soft. Add the peas to the pan, along with the turmeric and the remaining ½ teaspoon of salt. Stir around to distribute the turmeric and add a couple of tablespoons of water. If you prefer a more mashed consistency, you could use a fork to squash the beans a little. Allow to warm through for 5 minutes or so, then serve with buttered rice or a *palata* (see page 164).

Storage notes
The boiled peas, whether sautéed or not, can be stored in an airtight container for 3–4 days.

Kyet thar athe

STIR-FRIED SPICY CHICKEN LIVERS

Serves 4 as a side, 2 as a main

6 tbsp oil (vegetable, sunflower
   or peanut)
1 medium onion, chopped
3 garlic cloves, finely chopped
½ thumb-sized piece of ginger,
   peeled and crushed
2 tsp turmeric powder
1 tsp paprika
1–2 tsp chilli powder
400g chicken livers, chopped
   into 2cm chunks
1 tbsp fish sauce

Chicken livers are so underrated – they're cheap, full of flavour and very quick to cook. Offal and tripe are very popular in Burma, whether it be on barbecued skewers or in a 'hot pot' with broth. We think even those a little wary of liver could be persuaded by this dish. Serve this with rice and ideally a salad, to cut through the richness – we would recommend the ginger salad on page 54.

Heat the oil in a wok or large frying pan over a medium-high heat. Fry the onion in the pan until soft – this should take about 5 minutes – stirring occasionally to prevent sticking or burning. Turn down the heat to low-medium, add the garlic and ginger and fry for 1 minute. Add the spices and stir the mixture for a further minute.

Pat the livers dry with kitchen paper, then add them to the pan and stir-fry for 8–10 minutes, until they are just cooked. Add the fish sauce and taste – adjust the chilli level according to your preference.

NOODLES

ခေါက်ဆွဲ

NOODLES

There is a vast array of noodle dishes in Burma, and when you include regional variations, the list is endless. They can be eaten at any point during the day, including breakfast, and to us there is no better way to start the day. *Mohinga* (see pages 88–91) is probably the most famous one and is our mum's absolute favourite. We have two versions: one for more everyday occasions, which is made using tinned fish, and another made using the authentic catfish, which is slightly more time-consuming but results in a meatier broth. *Ohn no khauk swe* (coconut chicken noodles, see page 86) is the dish we make most often, we would have it for birthdays or for New Year's parties in huge quantities, and we would guess that every single friend we have cooked for has sampled it by now.

In comparison, *nangyi thoke* (rice noodles with chicken, see page 92) and *khauk swe thoke* (noodle salad, see page 60) are drier dishes that are typically eaten at room temperature alongside crispy garnishes and garlic oil.

Noodles have always played a big part in our lives, due to our Chinese and Burmese heritage. Dad instilled the Chinese superstition of the importance of having noodles on birthdays to ensure a long life. It was deemed so essential that no matter what we had planned on our birthdays, he would encourage us to sneak in a bowl of instant noodles at the very least!

Ohn no khauk swe

COCONUT CHICKEN NOODLES

Serves 6

This is one of our favourite dishes; it is lightly spiced, comforting, rich with coconut and it certainly leaves an impression. We often make a big batch of this for parties, specifically birthdays – Dad was a firm believer in the Chinese tradition of having noodles for good luck on your birthday! Guests can adjust their bowls to their own tastes by adding various multi-textured garnishes and condiments from a selection on the table.

5 tbsp oil (vegetable, sunflower or peanut), plus extra for browning the chicken
5 medium onions, chopped
10 garlic cloves, peeled
2 thumb-sized pieces of ginger, peeled
8 skinless and boneless chicken thighs, chopped into 3cm pieces
2 tbsp paprika
1 tsp turmeric powder
2 tsp chilli powder
100g creamed coconut (the solid block type), or 200ml coconut milk would work
2 tbsp gram flour, toasted (see page 203)
600ml chicken stock
2–3 tbsp fish sauce
400ml cold water

To serve
6 nests (450–500g) dried chow mein or egg noodles, cooked
3 limes, cut into wedges
6 hard-boiled eggs, cut in half
Coriander leaves
4 shallots, thinly sliced
1 batch of crispy fried rice noodles (see page 155)
Chilli flakes or chilli oil
Fish sauce

Heat the oil in a large casserole dish set over a medium heat. Add the chopped onions and cook slowly, turning down the heat to low-medium and stirring every 4–5 minutes until softened and starting to lightly brown in colour and become oily but not crispy – this should take about 15 minutes.

Meanwhile, crush the garlic cloves and ginger to a paste using a pestle and mortar, or blitz in a food processor.

Once the onions are ready, add the garlic and ginger paste and fry for 2 minutes to release the gorgeous flavours. Add a splash more oil, then brown the chicken pieces with the onion/garlic/ginger mix. Add the spices and creamed coconut, breaking it up into smaller pieces as you stir – it should melt. Stir in the toasted gram flour, followed by the chicken stock, fish sauce and the cold water. Bring to the boil and allow to simmer, uncovered, over a low, gentle heat for about 30 minutes. If the broth is too thick, add some water.

Serve hot on a bed of cooked egg noodles. Add a squeeze of lime juice and top with boiled eggs and the remaining garnishes in little bowls for everyone to help themselves to.

Storage notes
This chicken curry can be made in advance and stored in the fridge for up to 4 days. It can also be frozen for up to 3 months.

Mohinga

AROMATIC FISH NOODLE SOUP – SIMPLE VERSION

Serves 4–6

This is probably Burma's national dish, and our version was *Guardian* restaurant critic Grace Dent's 'best thing I ate in 2017'. This fish noodle soup is traditionally eaten at breakfast, but is readily available as a 'snack' at any time of day on the streets of Burma. The best we've had was cheap as chips, for as little as 30p a bowl, and eaten as we sat on plastic stools at the side of the road. Typically it is made with a type of catfish we can't source easily in London, but Grandma has used pilchards as a substitute for years and it works brilliantly to replicate the flavour. *Mohinga* also usually contains sliced banana stem, but we tend to just add more whole shallots instead.

2 tbsp rice flour

6 garlic cloves, peeled

Thumb-sized piece of ginger, peeled

3 lemongrass stalks

6 tbsp oil (vegetable, sunflower or peanut)

3 medium onions, thinly sliced

1 tbsp paprika

2 tsp turmeric powder

1–2 tsp chilli powder

1 tsp shrimp paste (optional)

2–3 tbsp fish sauce, plus extra to season

400g tin of pilchards in brine NOT ketchup (if you can't find pilchards use tinned sardines)

300g shallots, peeled

Black pepper

To serve

400g dried rice vermicelli (0.8–1mm size), cooked, rinsed and left in cold water

3 limes, cut into wedges

Garlic oil (see page 202)

Chilli flakes or chilli flakes in oil

6 hard-boiled eggs, cut in half

Coriander leaves

1 batch of crispy chana dal crackers (see page 148), broken up

First prepare the rice flour. Toast it in a dry frying pan over a medium heat for 3–5 minutes, stirring occasionally. Tip the flour out onto a plate and set aside.

Crush the garlic and ginger to a paste using a pestle and mortar or blitz in a food processor. Cut off and discard the first 5cm of the thin end of the lemongrass stalks and remove the tough outer layer, then bash what remains with a pestle or rolling pin to release the flavours.

Heat the oil in a large casserole dish over a medium heat. Add the sliced onions and cook until soft, stirring occasionally, for 5 minutes. Add the crushed garlic and ginger mix and stir for 1 minute, then add the lemongrass stalks.

Add the spices, shrimp paste, if using, and fish sauce and stir well. Then add the contents of the pilchards tin, including the brine. Mash the fish then add the toasted rice flour and mix well to prevent it sticking to the bottom of the pan. Top up with 1.2 litres of water and add the whole peeled shallots. Bring to the boil and simmer gently for 1 hour, uncovered, stirring occasionally.

Once cooked, remove the lemongrass, add a good grinding of black pepper and adjust the seasoning with a little fish sauce.

Put some drained rice noodles into each individual serving bowl, ladle over the soup, add a squeeze of lime, a drizzle of garlic oil, some chilli, as desired, and top with boiled eggs, coriander leaves and your broken up crackers. Serve immediately.

Storage notes

The fish soup can be made in advance and stored in the fridge for up to 4 days. It can also be frozen for up to 3 months.

Mohinga

AROMATIC FISH NOODLE SOUP – LONGER VERSION

Serves 8–10

Typically *mohinga* is made using catfish, which can be difficult to source. We have found you can get decent frozen ones from Asian supermarkets, usually in 1kg packets, so we have written the recipe to this amount. This longer version probably results in more meaty bits of fish and a greater depth of flavour (Mum would definitely prefer it) but in all honesty, day to day, we would happily make the simple version (see previous page) and save time.

For the first broth

1kg whole catfish, scaled and gutted
2 lemongrass stalks
Thumb-sized piece of ginger, peeled
1 garlic clove, peeled
1 tsp turmeric powder

For the soup

3 tbsp rice flour
10 garlic cloves
2 thumb-sized pieces of ginger, peeled
3 lemongrass stalks
8 tbsp oil (vegetable, sunflower or peanut)
6 medium onions, sliced
2 tbsp paprika
2 tbsp turmeric powder
2 tsp chilli powder
3 tbsp fish sauce, plus extra to season
500g shallots, peeled
Black pepper

To serve

800g dried rice vermicelli (0.8–1mm size), cooked, rinsed and left in cold water
6 limes, cut into wedges
Garlic oil (see page 202)
Chilli flakes or chilli flakes in oil
10 hard-boiled eggs, cut in half
Coriander leaves
2 batches of crispy chana dal crackers (see page 148), broken up

First prepare the rice flour. Toast it in a dry frying pan over a medium heat for 3–5 minutes, stirring occasionally. Tip the rice out onto a plate and set aside.

In a large pan or casserole dish that can hold at least 2 litres of liquid, place the catfish and other broth ingredients and pour in 1.5 litres of water, adding a bit more if needed, so the fish are submerged. Heat until the water is boiling, then lower the heat and simmer gently for 30 minutes, scooping away any scum that rises to the surface every so often.

Carefully remove the fish from the stock and place in a dish to allow to cool, straining the broth into a suitable container and discarding the lemongrass, etc.

Once the fish are cool enough to handle, carefully debone and reserve the flesh, including the skin (it pretty much melts away when you cook it). There are lots of fine bones so this can be a little time-consuming.

Clean up and dry your original pan ready to make the soup. Crush the garlic and ginger to form a paste using a pestle and mortar or blitz in a food processor. Cut off and discard the first 5cm of the thin end of the lemongrass stalks and remove the tough outer layer, then bash what remains with a pestle or rolling pin to release the flavours.

Heat the oil in your pan over a medium heat. Add the sliced onions and cook until soft, stirring occasionally, for 5 minutes. Add the crushed garlic and ginger mix and stir for a minute, then add the lemongrass stalks.

Add the spices and fish sauce and stir well, then add the reserved catfish flesh. Mash the fish then add the toasted rice flour and mix well to prevent it sticking to the bottom of the pan. Top up with the reserved catfish broth, add the peeled whole shallots and bring to the boil, then lower the heat and simmer for 45 minutes. Add more water if the soup seems too thick.

Remove the lemongrass stalks and adjust the seasoning with black pepper and fish sauce. Put some drained rice noodles into each individual serving bowl, ladle over the soup, add a squeeze of lime, a drizzle of garlic oil, some chilli, as desired, and top with boiled eggs, coriander leaves and your broken up crackers.

Storage notes
If you've been able to get hold of fresh catfish, the soup can be made in advance and stored in the fridge for up to 4 days. It can also be frozen for up to 3 months. However, if you've used pre-frozen catfish that you've defrosted you should eat this immediately.

Nangyi thoke

RICE NOODLES WITH CHICKEN

Serves 4

Nangyi refers to the type of thick, round rice noodles used in this dish, which perfectly complement this warming chicken curry and more of those textures that we love. Some have even likened this recipe to 'Burma's spaghetti'. We can't say we find this and Spag Bol that similar, but what they do share is they're both comforting and filling. We have also made a vegetarian version at our supper clubs, using chickpeas instead of chicken and seasoning it with vegetarian fish sauce. Udon noodles are a good substitute if you can't find *nangyi* noodles.

6 tbsp oil (vegetable, sunflower
   or peanut), plus extra for frying
   the chicken
3 medium onions, finely sliced
5 garlic cloves, finely chopped
1 tbsp paprika
2 tsp turmeric powder
1–2 tsp chilli powder
500g skinless and boneless chicken
   thighs, cut into 1–2cm chunks
1 tbsp fish sauce, plus extra to serve

To serve
400g rice noodles, cooked as per
   instructions, or 800g udon noodles
6–8 tbsp gram flour, toasted (see
   page 203)
Crispy fried garlic and garlic oil
   (see page 202)
4 hard-boiled eggs, sliced
Bunch of coriander, chopped
2 shallots, finely sliced
Chilli flakes
2 limes, cut into wedges

Heat the oil in a thick-bottomed pan or casserole dish set over a medium heat. Add the onions and fry until soft and golden, stirring every few minutes, then turn the heat down to allow them to cook slowly for 15–20 minutes, until you see the oil is rising.

Add the garlic and fry for 1 minute, then add the spices and stir for a further minute or so. Add another splash of oil, before frying off the chicken pieces in the fragrant mix, stirring it all well. Finally, add the fish sauce and 50ml of water to loosen the sauce, then cook for 10 minutes until the chicken is cooked through. Put some cooked rice noodles into each individual serving bowl, add a couple of spoons of the chicken curry, a spoon of gram flour, the crispy garlic and a drizzle of its oil, the sliced boiled eggs, coriander, a few slices of shallot, some chilli flakes, and finally a squeeze of lime juice. Mix well and enjoy.

Storage notes

This chicken curry and the noodles may be prepared in advance and stored in the fridge for up to 4 days. The curry may be frozen on the day of cooking for up to 3 months. Defrost carefully and reheat thoroughly when serving.

Panthay khauk swe

PANTHAY CHICKEN NOODLES

Serves 4

Panthay is a term used to describe the predominantly Muslim Hui people of China who migrated to Burma. *Panthay khauk swe* is a marriage of Indo-Chinese flavours served with Burmese-style garnishes, and it is a good example of how such popular dishes have evolved from different influences.

8 tbsp oil (vegetable, sunflower or peanut)
2 medium onions, chopped
6 garlic cloves
1 thumb-sized piece of ginger
500g skinless and boneless chicken thighs, cut into 2cm chunks
1 tsp chilli powder
1 tsp turmeric powder
1 tsp paprika
1 tsp ground coriander
2 tsp cumin powder
1 tbsp dark soy sauce

To serve
250g chow mein or egg noodles, cooked
2 hard-boiled eggs, cut in half
2 spring onions, finely sliced into rings
Chilli flakes
Crispy fried egg noodles (see page 155)

Heat the oil in a large lidded casserole dish set over a medium-high heat. Add the onions and cook slowly, turning down the heat to low-medium and stirring every 4–5 minutes until softened and starting to lightly colour and become oily – this should take at least 15 minutes.

While the onions are cooking, crush the garlic cloves and ginger to a paste using a pestle and mortar or blitz in a food processor. Once the onions are ready, add the crushed garlic and ginger and fry for 1 minute until fragrant. Add the chicken pieces and stir to brown evenly, then tip in the spices and the dark soy sauce and stir-fry for a few minutes, before adding a couple of tablespoons of water to loosen the sauce. Allow to simmer for 10 minutes, until the chicken is cooked through.

Serve hot on a bed of cooked noodles and garnish each bowl with half a boiled egg, some spring onions, chilli flakes and the crispy noodles.

Storage notes
This chicken curry can be stored in a container in the fridge for up to 4 days or frozen on the day of cooking for up to 3 months. Defrost carefully and reheat thoroughly when serving. The noodles are best prepared and eaten fresh on the day.

Shan khauk swe

SHAN NOODLES
Serves 4

A light dish, often munched in a tea shop for breakfast or as a snack later in the day. This comes in both a dry and a more broth-y version; we tend to prefer the former, but you could always add a bit of stock if you like. We had our first memorable taste of this dish when we visited Inle Lake, in the Shan Hills of Burma, at a simple roadside café. We went back twice!

2 tbsp oil (vegetable, sunflower or peanut), plus extra for frying

1 medium onion, chopped

4 garlic cloves, peeled and finely chopped

1 tsp paprika

1 tsp chilli powder

2 tbsp yellow soy bean paste (if you can't get hold of this, use 2 tbsp light soy sauce and 1 tsp tomato ketchup)

500g skinless chicken thighs or pork shoulder (or quorn mince), cut into 1cm chunks

200g fresh or tinned tomatoes, chopped

1 tsp fish sauce or vegetarian fish sauce (optional)

To serve

100g unsalted roasted peanuts

400g rice noodles (thin bun kho 1.2mm vermicelli or wide pho 3mm/pad Thai style), cooked

4 spring onions, green tips thinly sliced

Garlic oil (page 202)

Chilli flakes

Pickled mustard greens, finely chopped (see page 29)

Crispy pork rinds (optional, sometimes sold in bags labelled 'chicharon')

Heat the oil in a frying pan or wok over a medium heat. Add the chopped onion and cook, stirring, until soft and starting to colour – this should take about 5 minutes. Add a splash more oil and the garlic and stir for 1 minute. Add the spices and soy bean paste, then toss in the meat or quorn mince, allowing it to brown gently. Add the chopped tomatoes, 200ml of water and the fish sauce, if using. Bring to a gentle simmer and leave to cook for 10 minutes over a low heat, uncovered.

Meanwhile, crush the peanuts in a pestle and mortar or pulse in a food processor to a rough texture. Set aside.

Assemble individual bowls with drained rice noodles and a couple of spoons of your tomato sauce, and top with spring onions, crushed peanuts, a drizzle of garlic oil and a pinch of chilli flakes. Traditionally these are also served with some chopped preserved mustard greens and a couple of crispy pork rinds.

Storage notes
The sauce and noodles may be prepared in advance and stored in the fridge for up to 4 days. The sauce may be frozen on the day of cooking for up to 3 months. Defrost carefully and reheat thoroughly when serving.

Hsi jet khauk swe

GARLIC OIL NOODLES

Serves 4

75ml oil (vegetable, sunflower or
    peanut)
5 garlic cloves, peeled and finely
    chopped
500g pork belly slices, thinly sliced
    (0.5cm thick)
200ml pork or vegetable stock
4 nests of dried chow mein or egg
    noodles (about 300g total)
2 tbsp light soy sauce, plus extra
    (optional)
2 spring onions, thinly sliced

This is a really simple dish, perfect for midweek, and it doesn't take long to prepare. You could use any leftover roast meat instead of the pork belly in the recipe, or even omit it entirely.

First, make some garlic oil. Have a heatproof bowl ready. Heat the oil in a saucepan or wok over a medium-high heat and fry the garlic for a few minutes until it is crispy and golden, then quickly pour the garlic and oil into the bowl.

Without washing out the pan, return it to a medium heat and add the pork belly and stock, cover the pan with a lid and leave to braise for 15 minutes.

Meanwhile, cook the noodles in a large pan as per the packet instructions, then drain and return them to the pan you cooked them in, which will retain some heat.

The pork should now be cooked and tender. Strain it, reserving the cooking stock, and add the meat to the noodles, plus the garlic oil, soy sauce, 2 tablespoons of cooking stock and spring onions. Mix well and taste, adjust the seasoning with more soy sauce if needed and add more stock if you like more sauce.

Storage notes
All components may be prepared in advance and can be stored in the fridge, in separate containers, for up to 3–4 days, then combined and reheated.

CURRIES AND STEWS

ဆီပြန်ဟင်း

CURRIES AND STEWS

The beauty of most of the dishes in this section is that once prepared they can be left alone for an hour or two to slow-cook and develop deep flavours and tenderness with zero effort. Another convenient bonus is that once cooked, they can be cooled and refrigerated, then reheated a few days later, having matured and enhanced in flavour – perfect for batch cooking or entertaining when you know you have a busy week ahead.

We have opened this section with some advice on cooking onions. This was a piece we wrote early on in our journey with this book as it is absolutely at the heart of so many of our main dishes. Not long after, we encountered the wonderful Asma Khan's cookbook and we were overjoyed that she too featured a section specifically on this topic. Onions, oh beautiful onions! They are so important as the base of most curries and stews. We grew up with the familiar sight of an orange-netted sack full of onions, sitting in a basket in the corner of the kitchen, the discarded skins constantly drifting over the floor and being swept up onto the bottom of your sock, and eyes watering as you walk in on Mum peeling and chopping a huge pile of them. Then, finally, we would smell the sweet and comforting aroma of delicious fried onions!

The dishes in this chapter conjure up some of our favourite childhood food memories. Whether it's Mum's *bazun hin* (see page 114), the delectable prawn curry which was always a winner at a family party, served with rice and a spread of different salads and relishes; or a simple dinner of leftover *ame hnat* (see page 109), a tender beef curry spread onto a piece of buttered white toast; or simply a big pan of simmering *dal* (see page 126), ready to be dived into with a crispy flatbread.

We can't talk about Burmese curries without mentioning oil. If you've been to Burma, you will have noticed that there is often a golden layer of oil on top of their curries. One of the main reasons for this is preservation, as historically refrigeration was not always available, and the oil would keep the pathogens away. This oil is intensely flavoursome, developed during the cooking of onions and garlic. You know when a curry is ready when the 'oil rises' – or *sipyan*. It can always be skimmed away if you prefer.

Kyethun kyaw chet ni

COOKING ONIONS

The base of several of our dishes involves the slow, gentle cooking of a large – and at times ridiculous – amount of onions. In Burma you would use smaller, more shallot-like pink alliums than those we use in the UK. These cooked, oily onions that we call 'onion mix' add a deep, slightly sweet flavour to contrast with the other elements of our dishes. As there are so many to chop up, it's absolutely fine to use a food processor to get your onions chopped and make your life easier. Use whatever onions you like here – big, small, red, white, brown, or shallots. Our recipes refer to 'medium' onions (with their skin on they weigh 110–130g each) but please don't get bogged down with being too specific, as an extra onion never did a dish any harm! Both of us are significantly short-sighted and used to wear gas permeable i.e. 'hard' contact lenses. The one advantage of these is that your eyes become immune to onion-induced tears (unfortunately this has since returned because we have both had laser eye surgery!).

Usually one of us gets the onion job prior to a supper club – it's not popular as there are so many onions and it's hot and you're left smelling extremely fragrant. In Burma it would be done in the external part of the kitchen, which sadly we don't have the luxury of here. The best thing to do is to close the door and ventilate the room if you are making a large batch.

When cooking them, you need to use plenty of oil. Don't be afraid of oil, it adds flavour, but if it does bother you, any excess oil can be removed at the end if you so desire. If you plan on making several dishes you could make a large batch of cooked onion mix and freeze the spare portions in bags, where they can be stored for up to 3 months. When you need them, defrost them completely, then fry them off with the other ingredients according to your recipe. Or you can use this mix for non-Burmese dishes – be it the base of stews, curries or stir-fries, topping a steak or a burger ... or even in a quiche. The list goes on! Your individual recipes will specify the amount of oil and onions you will need, but here you'll get a batch that could be used to make a stew or curry for about four people.

6–8 tbsp oil (vegetable, sunflower
    or peanut)
4 medium onions, diced

Heat the oil in a casserole or thick-bottomed pan set over a medium heat. Add the chopped onions but do not overcrowd the pan – a layer 2cm deep is enough or they'll end up steaming rather than frying. You may need to do this in batches if you are making a large batch.

Stir the onions, lowering the heat to low-medium. You want them gently sizzling and colouring slowly. If they are starting to stick to the bottom of the pan, add a splash more oil and give them a good stir around. We usually set an alarm to stir and check on them every 5 minutes or so while prepping other bits and bobs. It will take at least 15 minutes, maybe even as long as 25, for them to be done – they will be soft, light-brown in colour and oily, as the water content from the onions will have evaporated. The oil takes on a wonderful onion flavour, so don't be afraid of it.

Storage notes

The prepared onions can be stored in a sealed container in the fridge for up to 4 days or frozen on the day of cooking for up to 3 months. Defrost carefully and reheat thoroughly before serving.

Cook's notes

We never use olive oil for this, both due to its flavour and its low burning point, which is not ideal when frying onions for a long time.

Wet nan yo pe hin

SPARE RIB AND DAL CURRY

Serves 3–4

You won't find this in a typical Burmese restaurant; in reality, it's entirely made up by Grandma, definitely Indian-influenced but mainly just utterly delicious and a true revelation when Mum introduced us to it. It's best made with short, stubby and meaty pork ribs, if you can get them, rather than skinny loin ribs, but they of course will do the job if that's all you can get. Beef ribs would also work a treat, but as they're bigger they would need a longer cooking time. You can use chana dal or yellow split peas here; if you are using split peas, the result will be softer and more mushy, whereas chana dal tends to hold its shape and texture.

3 tbsp oil (vegetable, sunflower or peanut)
1 medium onion, chopped
3 garlic cloves, peeled and thinly sliced
1 thumb-sized piece of ginger, peeled and crushed
1kg pork ribs, divided into individual ribs
1 tbsp mild curry powder
1 tsp ground cumin
1 tsp medium chilli powder
1 tsp salt
100g chana dal or yellow split peas, soaked in water for 4 hours or overnight
400ml coconut milk

Heat the oil in a casserole dish or a large, thick-bottomed, lidded saucepan over a medium-high heat. Fry the onion until it is starting to soften, stirring occasionally to prevent it sticking – this should take about 5 minutes.

Add the garlic and ginger to the pan and fry for 1 minute, then add the ribs to the pan and brown them gently, turning the heat to low-medium. Add the spices and salt and stir around to coat the meat. Add the drained chana dal to the pan and mix everything well.

Pour in the coconut milk and bring to a gentle simmer. Cover the pan and leave to cook for about 45 minutes, stirring occasionally to prevent sticking. If the sauce is too thick for your liking, add up to 100ml of water.

Check that the pork is tender and adjust the seasoning if necessary, then serve with rice.

Storage notes
This curry can be stored in a container in the fridge for up to 4 days. Reheat thoroughly before serving.

Kyet u hin

EGG CURRY

Serves 4

Egg curry is sometimes thought of as a last resort, a store cupboard standby when you have nothing else in the house. It has long spent time out of the limelight, but it needs to become more of a star dish, and a dish made with enthusiasm, in our opinion. It's simple, delicious and nutritious and is a firm favourite in our family. For extra indulgence, make this with duck eggs.

5 tbsp oil (vegetable, sunflower or peanut)

2 tsp turmeric powder

8 hard-boiled eggs (see Cook's notes)

2 medium onions, finely chopped

3 garlic cloves, crushed

1 tsp paprika

1 tsp medium chilli powder

Black pepper

2 tbsp fish sauce (omit for vegetarians; season with salt)

200g fresh or tinned tomatoes, chopped

2 tbsp tamarind water (see page 204 or substitute with ½ tsp tamarind concentrate stirred into 50ml warm water)

Handful of chopped coriander, to garnish

Heat the oil in a large frying pan set over a medium-high heat. Add a smidge of turmeric, and if it starts sizzling, it's ready. Add all the turmeric and stir to distribute evenly.

Gently place your boiled eggs into the yellow oil and fry until golden on all sides, turning them to ensure even colouring. The surface of the eggs may start to bubble and blister, which is fine. This will take 5–7 minutes. Carefully remove the eggs and leave them on a plate on the side.

Now fry the onions in the turmeric oil left in the pan. Turn down the heat to allow them to sizzle and fry gently until softened and starting to brown, stirring occasionally, for about 15 minutes (see cooking onions, page 102).

Add the garlic and stir for 1 minute, then add the paprika, chilli powder, a good grinding of black pepper and the fish sauce and mix well. Add the chopped tomatoes, tamarind water and 100ml of water and allow everything to come to a gentle boil. Cut the boiled eggs in half and add them to the curry sauce. Stir gently to get the eggs saucy but try not to poke the yolks out of their whites. Allow to simmer for 10 minutes, then serve with rice and garnish with fresh coriander.

Cook's notes

Everyone has their own method for boiling eggs; we put them in a pan, cover them with cold water and cook over a medium heat until boiling vigorously, then turn the heat down and set a timer for 7 minutes. Drain and rinse the eggs under the cool tap for a few minutes, allow to cool for 5 minutes or so, then peel.

Storage notes

This curry can be stored for up to 4 days in the fridge and then reheated. Never freeze boiled eggs; they develop a terrible texture!

Wet tha ni a cho hin

RED PORK STEW

Serves 4 generously, 6 as
a side

The best *wet tha ni a cho hin* we had was cooked by our friend Kim May Ohn, whose father was the late, great musician, U Ant Gyi, whom we had the pleasure of meeting in 2014. This is a gently spiced dish of meltingly soft pork which glows red – hence the name.

For the marinade

1kg pork belly, rind removed, flesh cut
 into large chunks
10 garlic cloves, peeled
2 thumb-sized pieces of ginger, peeled
3 tbsp kecap manis (thick, sweet soy
 sauce)
2 tbsp white vinegar

For the stew

5 tbsp oil (vegetable, sunflower
 or peanut)
2 tbsp caster sugar
1 tsp medium chilli powder
2 tsp paprika
1 tbsp fish sauce
12 shallots, peeled

Place the pork belly chunks in a large container that will fit in the fridge. Crush the garlic and ginger to a paste using a pestle and mortar or blitz in a food processor. Place half the paste in the container with the pork pieces and add the kecap manis and vinegar. Mix, ideally with your hands, so that the meat gets evenly coated. Cover the container and leave it in the fridge for at least an hour (or overnight is fine). Keep the remaining ginger/garlic paste aside, covered, in the fridge.

When you are ready to cook the meat, preheat the oven to 180° C/350° F/gas mark 4.

Put an ovenproof casserole dish over a medium heat on the hob and add the oil and sugar. Stir, and cook until the sugar starts sizzling.

Add the pork and allow it to brown and caramelise, turning the heat to low, for 2–3 minutes. Then turn the pork pieces over to cook on the other side for another couple of minutes. Add the remaining ginger/garlic paste and stir for a minute.

Add the chilli powder, paprika, fish sauce and 500ml of water and stir well. Let the liquid come to the boil, then cover the dish and put it in the oven for 1 hour. After an hour, give the stew a stir, add some more water if it's looking dry and add the whole shallots. Put the stew back in the oven for a further 30 minutes.

Once cooked, remove from the oven – the pork should be tender. The gravy might be oily and on the thin side, but don't worry, this is normal. Taste and adjust the seasoning as required, then serve with plenty of rice.

Storage notes

This stew can be stored in a sealed container in the fridge for up to 4 days or frozen on the day of cooking for up to 3 months. Defrost carefully and reheat thoroughly before serving.

Ame hnat

BEEF CURRY
Serves 4

This is a comforting dish that can be served simply with fluffy steamed rice and one of our fresh, tangy salads to complement its richness. You might be surprised by the amount of oil that comes to the surface as this cooks, but that is how it should be. The oil is richly flavoured, but if it really bothers you, you can just scoop it away. Venison would also work wonderfully well in this recipe.

200ml oil (vegetable, sunflower
   or peanut)
800g boneless beef shin
5 medium onions, chopped
10 garlic cloves, peeled
1 thumb-sized piece of ginger,
   peeled
½ bunch of coriander stalks,
   finely chopped
2 tsp paprika
2 tsp turmeric powder
1 tsp medium chilli powder
2–3 tbsp fish sauce
600ml beef stock

Preheat the oven to 160° C/325° F/gas mark 3.

Heat 2 tablespoons of the oil in a large ovenproof casserole dish over a medium heat. Sear the pieces of beef shin until golden brown, then set them aside in a bowl.

In the same casserole dish, heat the rest of the oil over a medium heat. Add the chopped onions and cook slowly, turning down the heat to low-medium and stirring every 4–5 minutes until softened and starting to lightly colour and become oily – this will take at least 15 minutes (see cooking onions, page 102).

While the onions are cooking, crush the garlic cloves and ginger to a paste using a pestle and mortar, or blitz in a food processor.

Once the onions are ready, add the crushed garlic, ginger and coriander stalks to the dish and fry for a few minutes until fragrant. Add all the spices and the beef and stir well to coat. Pour in the fish sauce and beef stock and stir – the liquid should just cover the top of the beef, if not, just add more water. Bring to the boil, cover with a lid, then place the dish in the oven for 2 hours, by which point the meat should be beautifully tender. Check halfway through, to ensure there is still some liquid in the dish, and if required, top up with water.

Serve hot with rice.

Storage notes
This curry can be stored in a sealed container in the fridge for up to 4 days or frozen on the day of cooking for up to 3 months. Defrost carefully and reheat thoroughly before serving.

Ngar Hin

FISH CURRY

Serves 4

A fragrant, mildly spiced curry which can be made using any firm, meaty white fish, such as cod, pollock, haddock or coley. Be sure to use large chunks and try not to over-stir during cooking so that the pieces remain intact. It is possible to make the curry sauce in advance – simply reheat it prior to serving, then add the fish and cook it through.

500g firm white fish, skin removed and cut into 5cm chunks
6 garlic cloves, peeled
½ thumb-sized piece of ginger, peeled
8 tbsp oil (vegetable, sunflower or peanut)
3 medium onions, chopped
2 tsp paprika
1 tsp turmeric powder
1 tsp medium chilli powder
2–3 tbsp fish sauce
4 medium tomatoes, chopped

For the marinade
1½ tsp turmeric powder
1 tsp salt

To serve
Coriander leaves (optional)
Crispy fried shallots (shop-bought or see page 200)

First make the marinade. Combine the turmeric and salt in a bowl, then add the fish chunks and turn to coat them in the marinade. Transfer to the fridge to marinate for 30 minutes.

Meanwhile, crush the garlic cloves and ginger to a paste using a pestle and mortar or blitz in a food processor.

Heat the oil over a medium heat in a large casserole dish. Add the chopped onions and cook slowly, turning the heat down to low-medium and stirring every 4–5 minutes until softened and starting to colour lightly and become oily – this will take at least 15 minutes (see cooking onions, page 102). Once the onions are ready, add the crushed garlic and ginger and fry for a few minutes until fragrant.

Add the spices, fish sauce and chopped tomatoes, breaking them up slightly as you stir. Allow to simmer for 5–10 minutes (If you want to get ahead, you could make the sauce up to this point then store in the fridge until you're ready to cook the fish.) Add the fish and 100ml of water. Bring to the boil and cover with a lid, then simmer over a low heat for 5–10 minutes until the fish is cooked.

Garnish with coriander leaves, if you like, and the crispy shallots for added texture.

Storage notes
This curry can be stored in a container in the fridge for up to 4 days or frozen on the day of cooking for up to 3 months. Defrost carefully and reheat thoroughly before serving.

Kyet tha aloo hin

CHICKEN POTATO CURRY

Serves 4

Who doesn't love a fried potato? And the potato in this curry is deep-fried before being added to the chicken to give it an extra bit of texture and flavour. You could even make this a vegetarian potato curry by replacing the chicken with some extra vegetables such as cauliflower, carrots or beans, and omitting the fish sauce.

2 tbsp gram flour

1 tsp salt

2 large potatoes, peeled and chopped into 2–5cm chunks

Oil (vegetable, sunflower or peanut), for deep-frying potatoes, plus 6 tbsp and a little extra for browning the chicken

3 medium onions, chopped

6 garlic cloves, peeled

1 thumb-sized piece of ginger, peeled

6 skinless and boneless chicken thighs, cut into 5cm chunks

2 tsp paprika

1 tsp turmeric powder

2 tsp medium chilli powder

4 medium tomatoes, roughly chopped

2–3 tbsp fish sauce

Handful of coriander leaves, to garnish (optional)

Combine the gram flour and salt and coat the potatoes in it lightly. Line a plate with a few sheets of kitchen paper.

Pour the oil into a wok or heavy-based frying pan to a depth of 5cm and deep-fry the potatoes until golden brown. Make sure you don't overcrowd the pan. Scoop out the potato chunks using a heatproof strainer or sieve and transfer to the kitchen paper.

Heat the 6 tablespoons of oil in a large casserole dish set over a medium heat. Add the chopped onions and cook slowly, turning down the heat to low-medium and stirring every 4–5 minutes until softened and starting to colour lightly and become oily – this will take at least 15 minutes (see cooking onions, page 102).

Meanwhile, crush the garlic cloves and ginger to a paste using a pestle and mortar or blitz in a food processor. Once the onions are ready, add the crushed garlic and ginger and fry for a few minutes until fragrant.

Add a splash more oil, then brown the chicken pieces with the onion/garlic/ginger mix. Add the spices, tomatoes and fish sauce and stir for a few minutes until the tomatoes have broken down slightly. Add the deep-fried potatoes with 80ml of water and mix well. Leave to cook over a low-medium heat for 15–20 minutes, uncovered.

Serve with steamed rice, garnished with coriander leaves.

Storage notes
This curry can be stored in a container in the fridge for up to 4 days or frozen on the day of cooking for up to 3 months. Defrost carefully and reheat thoroughly before serving.

Bazun hin

PRAWN CURRY
Serves 4

This is a firm favourite in our family, often made by Mum. It is fairly quick to cook once the curry base has been made – and this can be prepared in advance quite easily – and if you have a bag of prawns in the freezer it is a handy last-minute fix. Burmese curries don't traditionally contain coconut but this is Mum's special addition to the recipe and we think it adds extra depth and an almost nutty flavour. It is still delicious if you skip this, though.

6 tbsp oil (vegetable, sunflower or peanut)

3 medium onions, chopped

10 garlic cloves, peeled

½ thumb-sized piece of ginger, peeled

½ bunch of coriander stalks, finely chopped, plus some leaves to garnish

2 tsp paprika

1 tsp turmeric powder

2 tsp medium chilli powder

50g creamed coconut (use the solid block type, or 50ml coconut milk would work too)

2–3 tbsp fish sauce

600g large, raw king prawns, peeled and deveined

Heat the oil in a large casserole dish or wok set over a medium-high heat. Add the chopped onions and cook slowly, turning down the heat to low-medium, and stirring every 4–5 minutes until softened and starting to colour lightly and become oily – this will take at least 15 minutes (see cooking onions, page 102).

While the onions are cooking, crush the garlic cloves and ginger to a paste using a pestle and mortar, or blitz in a food processor.

Once the onions are ready, add the crushed garlic, ginger and coriander stalks and fry for a few minutes until fragrant. Add the spices and creamed coconut, breaking it up into smaller pieces as you stir. It should melt in. Finally, add the fish sauce and the prawns and cook over a medium heat for about 5 minutes or until the prawns are cooked through.

Serve hot on steamed rice and garnish with coriander leaves.

Storage notes
We don't find the prawns reheat very well once cooked in the curry, but you could cook the sauce up until adding the prawns, then store in the fridge for up to 4 days, then just reheat and continue from adding the prawns.

Cook's note
Sometimes we use whole, shell-on prawns which look visually appealing and will make the curry more flavourful (we like to suck the heads!). Just increase the total weight to 800g–1kg to allow for the heads and shells.

Wet thar thayet thee the hnat hin

PORK AND MANGO PICKLE CURRY

Serves 4

This is one of our grandma's recipes, which has a lovely sour, spicy quality and is remarkably easy. You could make your own green mango pickle if you were feeling energetic, but the ready-made stuff is great and considerably less effort and expense – just be mindful that there may be pieces of mango bark in these jars, so either warn your guests or try to remove them prior to cooking.

5 tbsp oil (vegetable, sunflower or peanut), plus extra for browning the pork
3 medium onions, chopped
5 garlic cloves, peeled
1 thumb-sized piece of ginger, peeled
500g pork shoulder, cut into 3cm pieces
1 tbsp paprika
1 tsp turmeric powder
1 tsp medium chilli powder
2 tsp medium curry powder
1 tbsp fish sauce
150g green mango pickle (the brand Ahmed is good – this is about half a jar)

Heat the oil in a casserole dish or thick-bottomed, large, lidded saucepan over a medium heat. Add the onions and fry until soft and beginning to colour, stirring occasionally, for at least 10 minutes.

While the onions are cooking, crush the garlic cloves and ginger to a paste using a pestle and mortar, or blitz in a food processor. When the onions are ready, add this paste to the dish, then stir for a minute until the flavours are released.

Add a splash of oil to the dish and toss in the pork shoulder pieces, turning them as they cook until they are evenly browned, then add the spices, fish sauce and mango pickle and stir until well mixed. Add 300ml of water and bring to the boil, then cover, lower the heat and allow to simmer for 1 hour.

Check the pork is tender, then adjust the seasoning and add more fish sauce if you think it needs it (though it should be fairly well salted already) and serve with plenty of rice.

Storage notes

This pork curry can be stored in a container in the fridge for up to 4 days or frozen on the day of cooking for up to 3 months. Defrost carefully and reheat thoroughly before serving.

Shwe payon thee hin

PUMPKIN CURRY

Serves 4 as a main

We made a version of this dish for a collaborative supper club with our good friend Sirichai Kularbwong, who runs the incredible Thai restaurant Singburi, in Leytonstone. We learned a lot from him and his cooking and we both have wonderful memories of that evening, which meant eating some of the best food we have ever had. This is a delicious way to cook pumpkin or squash.

6 tbsp oil (vegetable, sunflower or peanut)

2 medium onions, chopped

5 garlic cloves, peeled

1 thumb-sized piece of ginger, peeled

1 tsp turmeric powder

2 tsp chilli powder

1 cinnamon stick

1 batch of tamarind water (see page 204)

1 tbsp light soy sauce

300ml vegetable stock

850g peeled pumpkin (kabocha is good) or butternut squash, cut into 3cm chunks

Heat the oil in a large lidded casserole dish over a medium-high heat. Add the chopped onions and cook slowly, turning down the heat to low-medium, and stirring every 4–5 minutes until softened and starting to colour lightly and become oily – this will take at least 15 minutes (see cooking onions, page 102).

While the onions are cooking, crush the garlic and ginger to a paste using a pestle and mortar, or blitz in a food processor.

Once the onions are soft and browned, add the crushed garlic and ginger and fry for a minute until fragrant, followed by the turmeric, chilli powder and cinnamon stick, stirring well for a further minute. Add the tamarind water, soy sauce, stock and pumpkin chunks. Bring to a gentle simmer and cook over a low heat, covered, for 25 minutes. Check a piece of pumpkin with a fork after this and if it's soft take the dish off the heat, otherwise continue cooking for another 5–10 minutes until the pieces are tender. The gravy is fairly thin, but you could reduce it further by cooking it, uncovered, if you prefer it thicker.

Check the seasoning and serve with rice.

Storage notes

This curry can be stored in a container in the fridge for up to 4 days or frozen on the day of cooking for up to 3 months. Defrost carefully and reheat thoroughly before serving.

Seik thar hin

MUTTON CURRY

Serves 4 generously

Mutton – the meat that comes from mature sheep, rather than lamb – has a great depth of flavour and is worth sourcing from a good butcher. In Burma this dish would be made with goat meat, so you could use this as an alternative. This is a dish that needs slow-cooking, but the time taken is worth it as you will be rewarded with a tender, unctuous crowd pleaser. We like to use mutton with a piece of bone, as it intensifies the flavours and releases rich marrow. Use big chunks, so that the pieces hold their integrity by the end of the slow-cook. Top tip: make a large batch and use the leftovers for mutton puffs (see page 159).

8 tbsp oil (vegetable, sunflower or peanut)
4 medium onions, chopped
6 garlic cloves, peeled
1 thumb-sized piece of ginger, peeled
½ bunch of coriander stalks, finely chopped, plus some leaves to garnish
2 tsp paprika
2 tsp turmeric powder
2 tsp chilli powder
1kg mutton shoulder (if you can get some bone to chuck in on top that's a bonus), cut into 3cm chunks
4 tbsp fish sauce
750ml hot water

Preheat the oven to 160° C/325° F/gas mark 3.

Heat the oil in an ovenproof lidded casserole dish set over a medium heat. Add the chopped onions and cook slowly, turning down the heat to low-medium and stirring every 4–5 minutes until softened and starting to colour lightly and become oily – this will take at least 15 minutes (see cooking onions, page 102).

Meanwhile, crush the garlic and ginger to a paste using a pestle and mortar, or blitz in a food processor.

Once the onions are soft and browned, add the ginger/garlic paste and coriander stalks and fry for a minute until fragrant. Add the spices and the mutton to the pan and mix well. Turn up the heat and stir the meat, cooking until it is browned evenly – this will take about 5 minutes.

Pour in the fish sauce with the hot water and stir. The liquid should just cover the top of the mutton, if not, add more water. Bring to the boil, then cover the pan and place it in the oven for 2½ hours, until you can easily pierce the mutton with a fork without resistance. Check after 1 hour of cooking to ensure there is still enough liquid in the dish, and top up if necessary (there should be enough to just cover the meat). The gravy will be on the runny side when the curry is done, but if you prefer it to be thicker, remove the meat from the curry and set the sauce over a high heat to reduce, then return the meat to the pan.

Serve hot with white rice and garnish with the coriander leaves.

Storage notes
This curry can be stored in an airtight container in the fridge for up to 4 days or frozen on the day of cooking for up to 3 months. Defrost thoroughly and ensure it is fully reheated before serving.

Khayan thee hin

AUBERGINE DAL CURRY

Serves 4

This is a great dish that happens to be vegan, which we found in one of Grandma's old recipe books. The frying of the dal in the flavoured oil creates a lovely nuttiness to the dish, which is particularly delicious alongside the chunks of tender aubergine and the creamy coconut sauce.

8 tbsp oil (vegetable, sunflower or peanut)

1 large aubergine, cut into bite-sized chunks

1 tsp black mustard seeds

1–2 green finger chillies

100g chana dal (yellow split peas)

2 tsp medium curry powder

1 tsp salt

100g creamed coconut (solid block type)

Coriander leaves, to garnish (optional)

Heat 5 tablespoons of the oil in a large lidded saucepan or casserole dish and fry the aubergine until slightly soft and nicely charred. Remove from the pan and keep aside.

Using the same pan over a medium heat, pour in the remaining oil and add the mustard seeds. Fry until you can hear them popping, then add the whole green chillies.

Add the chana dal and fry for a minute until slightly toasted in the oil. Be careful not to fry the dal for too long, as it may become hard and take longer to cook through. Add the curry powder, salt, creamed coconut and 500ml of water and bring to the boil. Return the fried aubergine to the pan and leave the curry to simmer very gently with the lid on for 1–1½ hours, stirring occasionally until the dal is tender. If the gravy seems too thick, you could add a little water.

Serve hot with steamed rice and garnish with fresh coriander leaves, if you like.

Storage notes

This curry can be stored in a container in the fridge for up to 4 days or frozen on the day of cooking for up to 3 months. Defrost carefully and reheat thoroughly before serving.

Magyi wet thar hin

PORK TAMARIND CURRY

Serves 6

Tamarind and palm sugar create a sweet and sour flavour in this curry, which makes it distinct from most of the other Burmese curries. This dish is best made using tamarind pulp but you can use tamarind concentrate instead. The pork could be replaced with beef if you prefer and it will be just as delicious.

150ml oil (vegetable, sunflower or peanut)
5 medium onions, chopped
8 garlic cloves
1 thumb-sized piece of ginger
1 green finger chilli
1 tsp paprika
1 tsp turmeric powder
½ tsp chilli powder
1 tbsp shrimp paste
1kg boneless pork shoulder, cut into 2.5cm chunks
3 batches of tamarind water (see page 204)
60g palm sugar

Heat the oil in a large casserole dish over a medium heat. Add the chopped onions and cook slowly, turning down the heat to low-medium, stirring every 4–5 minutes, until softened and starting to colour lightly and become oily – this will take at least 15 minutes (see cooking onions, page 102).

Meanwhile, crush the garlic, ginger and chilli to a paste using a pestle and mortar, or blitz in a food processor.

Once the onions are soft and lightly browned, add the crushed garlic, ginger and chilli and fry for a minute until fragrant. Add the spices and the shrimp paste and stir until the paste melts into the mixture.

Add the pork, then pour in the tamarind water with the palm sugar. Bring the curry to the boil and leave to simmer with the lid on for 1 hour, until the pork is tender. Stir the curry halfway through cooking and add some water if required.

Stir the curry well before serving up with steamed rice.

Storage notes
This pork curry can be stored in a container in the fridge for up to 4 days or frozen on the day of cooking for up to 3 months. Defrost carefully and reheat thoroughly before serving.

Khayan thee hnat

STUFFED AUBERGINE CURRY

Serves 4

In this dish we have tender baby aubergines stuffed with a strongly flavoured, shrimp-infused, spicy stuffing. You can use normal-sized aubergines if you can't get hold of the baby ones – they just need to be cooked for a bit longer. Unfortunately this dish isn't quite the same without the shrimp elements; it would still taste great but it would lack the umami kick.

2 tbsp dried shrimps
5 tbsp oil (vegetable, sunflower
    or peanut)
2 medium onions, finely chopped
5 garlic cloves, finely chopped
1 tsp chilli flakes
1 tsp turmeric powder
1 tsp paprika
1 tsp shrimp paste
8 long baby aubergines (about 500g)

To serve
Handful of crispy fried shallots
    (shop-bought or see page 200)
Handful of coriander leaves (optional)

Pound the dried shrimps to a powder using a pestle and mortar, or use a food processor.

Heat 4 tablespoons of the oil in a large lidded frying pan over a low-medium heat and cook the onion and garlic for about 10 minutes until soft and golden-coloured.

Add the chilli flakes, turmeric and paprika to the pan and stir for a minute or 2, until fragrant. Stir in the shrimp paste, so it melts into the mixture, add the shrimp powder and mix well, then empty the contents of the pan into a separate bowl.

Cut the aubergines in half along their length, but not all the way through, keeping the stem intact. Then make another cut along the length, again preserving the stem, so the aubergine is in quarters but still connected by the stem. Carefully 'fill' each aubergine with the mixture with your hands. This may get a bit messy and some of the filling may fall out, but that is fine. You should be left with a small amount of filling to add to the cooking sauce.

Give the used frying pan a bit of a wipe with kitchen paper, then heat the remaining oil in it over a high heat. Carefully add the aubergines. Try to turn them over carefully so that all sides are charred. This should take a couple of minutes. Add 150ml of water to the pan with the remaining filling and bring to the boil. Leave to simmer with a lid on.

After 15 minutes the aubergines should be soft and ready to serve. Garnish with the fried shallots and coriander.

Storage notes
This curry can be stored in a container in the fridge for up to 4 days or frozen on the day of cooking for up to 3 months. Defrost carefully and reheat thoroughly before serving.

Pe hin

DAL

Serves 4 as a main, 6 as a side

This is our standard midweek dal. It is such easy-to-make comfort food: nutritious, filling and cheap. We ate a lot of this when we were students … naturally. There are so many recipes for this out there, using different types of lentils and varying combinations of spices. Every family has their own recipe and rules, and here is our version.

250g chana dal (yellow split peas),
    soaked overnight or for at least
    4 hours
2 garlic cloves, peeled, left whole
6 tbsp vegetable oil
3 tsp cumin seeds
4 medium onions, finely sliced
1 tsp turmeric powder
1 tsp chilli powder
1½ tsp salt
Coriander leaves, to garnish (optional)

Rinse and drain the soaked chana dal, then add it to a pan with 1 litre of water. Add the garlic cloves, bring the dal to the boil and leave to simmer with a lid on for 1 hour, until soft. Make sure to stir from time to time and add more water if the dal looks like it might boil dry.

Meanwhile, heat the oil in a frying pan and add the cumin seeds. Fry for a minute or 2 until fragrant. Add the onions and fry slowly over a low heat until they are caramelised and slightly crispy. This should take 15–20 minutes. Set aside.

When the dal is cooked, add the turmeric, chilli powder and salt and use a spoon to gently mash the mixture with the cooked garlic until you get a thick, creamy consistency. Add some more water if you like your dal thinner.

Finally, when ready to serve, stir the fried cumin onions into the dal and serve garnished with coriander, if using.

Storage notes
This dal can be stored in a container in the fridge for up to 4 days or frozen on the day of cooking for up to 3 months. Defrost carefully and reheat thoroughly before serving.

RICE

ထမင်း

RICE

Rice is at the heart of every meal in Burma, and during the 1930s the country was the world's biggest exporter of the stuff. The national variety that is cultivated is called *paw hsan hmwe* and is known to be very fragrant with good texture and quality. Personally, we have always preferred to have plain steamed rice to accompany our Burmese feasts, but for those special occasions where you might want something a bit more indulgent, we have some suggestions here that are very simple to make, such as *ohn htamin* (coconut rice, see page 140) and *dhaw but htamin* (butter rice, see page 141).

There are lots of different methods for cooking rice and every family has their tried-and-tested way. We normally rinse the raw rice in a saucepan a couple of times, then top up with water so that the level comes up to double that of the rice (using a finger to measure). We then cover the pan and put this over a medium heat, until the water starts to boil and steam builds. We then turn the heat to low and leave for at least another ten minutes (or longer, depending on the volume cooking) until the water has absorbed. At this point you can test a grain to see if it is cooked. If so, take the pan off the heat and leave covered for five minutes before serving with the rest of your dishes.

Despite many years of cooking rice, we still struggle with estimating how much we need to cook, but if you have made too much, leftovers are perfect for making *htamin kyaw* (fried rice, see page 138) on another occasion. With rice, it is important that you cool it quickly then refrigerate it for no longer than a day before frying. Lastly, make sure you finish all the rice on your plate – every single grain – or else your future partner will be very unattractive (another classic Dad superstition).

Danbauk

BURMESE CHICKEN BIRYANI

Serves 6

Biryani is a dish originating from the Indian subcontinent and Persia, which has been adopted by Burma and one of the best places to eat it is at Nilar Biryani & Cold Drink in Yangon. It is labour-intensive, but we have tried to split it into the component parts and we promise you it's worth the effort. We have made this without saffron on occasion (not realising we didn't have it in the cupboard) and it was still delicious. Leftovers are also divine, by the way. Serve with some simple cucumber and tomato slices and plain yoghurt.

For the chicken marinade (marinate for at least 2 hours)
300g full-fat plain yoghurt
6 garlic cloves, peeled and finely chopped
½ thumb-sized piece of ginger, peeled and grated
1 tsp salt
Good sprinkling of black pepper
3 tsp turmeric powder
2 tsp ground cumin
1 tsp chilli powder

6 skinless whole chicken legs (not too big)

For the fried onions
3 tbsp oil (vegetable, sunflower or peanut)
3 tbsp butter
4 medium onions, sliced

For the chicken curry
3 garlic cloves, peeled
½ thumb-sized piece of ginger, peeled
Salt
3 tbsp oil (vegetable, sunflower or peanut)
1 tsp mustard seeds
2 cinnamon sticks
3 green cardamom pods, bashed

ingredients continued overleaf

Put all the marinade ingredients in a large container and mix well. Add the chicken and mix to ensure it is evenly coated, then cover and leave in the fridge for 2 hours or overnight.

While the chicken is marinating, prepare the fried onions. We love plenty of these. In a large saucepan, heat the oil and butter over a medium heat and once the butter is melted and starting to sizzle, add the sliced onions. You want to cook these slowly until browned and caramelised, so turn the heat down low and stir every few minutes for *at least* 15–20 minutes. Remove the onions when done and set aside. Don't wash this pan, as you can use it to make the chicken curry next.

Crush the garlic cloves and ginger to a coarse paste with a pinch of salt using a pestle and mortar. In the onion saucepan, add the 3 tablespoons of oil over a medium-high heat. Add the mustard seeds, cinnamon sticks, cardamom, black peppercorns and chilli powder and stir for a minute or 2; the mustard seeds will start popping and it will all start smelling fragrant, spiced and wonderful. Add the raw chopped onion to the pan and fry until soft and golden, turning the heat to low and stirring occasionally, for 5–10 minutes. Then add the garlic and ginger paste and stir for a minute, before letting the chicken legs join the party plus all the marinade, 1 teaspoon of salt and about 150ml of water. Stir well and bring to a gentle simmer. Allow to cook, covered, for 30 minutes or until the chicken is cooked through.

While the curry is cooking, prepare the rice; rinse it about three times in cold water then put it in a lidded saucepan with the chicken stock, cloves and 350ml of water and place over a low-medium heat. You want it JUST cooked, so check after 20 minutes and if the liquid has been absorbed and the grains are

continued overleaf

½ tsp black peppercorns

1 tsp chilli powder

1 medium onion, chopped

For the rice

750g basmati rice

500ml chicken stock

4 cloves

For assembly

Butter (about 100g total)

Pinch of saffron soaked in 2 tbsp
    warm milk or water

just tender, take the pan off the heat. If it's still hard, cook for a further few minutes.

Preheat the oven to 180° C/350° F/gas mark 4. Remove the chicken legs from the curry sauce and place on a plate. Keep the sauce for serving with the biriyani later. Now for the assembly. You need a large lidded ovenproof casserole dish. Grease with butter then place a third of the rice on the bottom, followed by a third of the fried onions, some dabs of butter, then three pieces of chicken. Top this with another third of the rice, a third of the fried onions, some more dabs of butter and the remaining chicken pieces, layering the top with the rest of the rice and onions and dabs of butter. Drizzle over the saffron-infused milk, put the lid on securely and cook for 25 minutes. Plate up the rice and serve a chicken leg on each, with the curry sauce on the side.

Cook's notes

The final stage of the recipe can also be cooked on the hob for the same duration; we've watched a video of the lovely Chetna Makan placing her cooking vessel into a large frying pan with some hot water in, to protect the bottom from catching.

Htamin let thoke

RICE (OR CARBFEST) SALAD

Serves 6

250ml boiling water

100g tamarind pulp

4 tbsp dried shrimps

3 tsp chilli oil (see page 210)

500g long-grain rice (raw weight),
    cooked

200g vermicelli noodles (raw weight),
    cooked

450g chow mein or egg noodles,
    cooked

750g white potatoes, peeled, boiled
    and sliced into 1cm rounds

100g gram flour, toasted (see page 203)

Garlic oil (see page 202)

Fish sauce

Chilli flakes

Storage notes
This dish is best prepared and eaten fresh on the day.

This is the ultimate 'salad', made up of no fewer than four different carbohydrates! When mixed with all the other ingredients it creates a dish full of flavour and texture. Every family has their own way of making it – some add cabbage, raw onion and even leftover chicken – so there are no fixed rules. Each person prepares their own plate and the beauty – but also the difficulty – of this dish is that no plate is the same and what you decide to mix together is up to you, depending on your personal taste. Amy's 'brand' tends to be slightly dark and on the sour side while Emily's is heavy on the garlic and chilli. One thing we have noticed over the years is how the first bowl is always the best!

In terms of the preparation, the different components should be made in advance as the cooked ingredients need be left to cool before serving this salad at room temperature. Once everything is ready, assemble it all on a table and crowd round. A good lie-down is recommended afterwards. (*Recipe pictured overleaf.*)

Make the tamarind water by adding the boiling water to the tamarind pulp in a heatproof bowl and leave to soak for a few minutes. Use a fork to further break up the pulp, then strain through a sieve, discarding any stones, so that you are left with the tamarind water.

Pound the dried shrimps to a powder using a pestle and mortar or use a food processor. Add the chilli oil to the cooked rice and mix well.

Assemble all the prepared components in separate bowls on the dining table. Each person will need a plate and can either use hands or cutlery to mash everything together. For each plate, add a handful of rice, a handful of the two types of noodles and 2–3 pieces of potato. Then add a teaspoon of shrimp powder, 1 tablespoon of gram flour, 1–2 tablespoons of garlic oil, 2–3 tablespoons of tamarind water, 1 tablespoon of fish sauce and chilli flakes as you fancy, then mix thoroughly, squidging the potatoes into mash.

Taste your mixture and adjust the seasoning according to your preference by adding more ingredients, such as fish sauce for saltiness, chilli for spice, tamarind for sourness, garlic for flavour and gram flour for nuttiness and texture. It should be on the moist side, but how much will depend on what *you* like!

Once you are happy, devour immediately.

Htamin kyaw

FRIED RICE

Serves 4

Fried rice is a classic store cupboard/fridge forage staple, and this recipe is absolutely flexible as to what you can add to it – any meat, prawns, tofu, Chinese sausage, leftover fried chicken… The key here is not to overload the pan you're cooking it in, so that the rice fries rather than steams. Ideally make this in a big wok.

3 tbsp oil (vegetable, sunflower
    or peanut)
2 spring onions, thinly sliced
1 garlic clove, peeled and thinly sliced
1 tbsp dried shrimps (optional)
750g leftover cooked and chilled rice,
    clumps broken up
Handful of leftover meat, bacon,
    ham or tofu, diced, or prawns
Small handful of frozen peas
Small handful of diced carrot
2 eggs
1 tsp fish sauce
1½ tbsp light soy sauce
Optional for garnish: fresh sliced chilli,
    handful of chopped coriander, crispy
    fried shallots (shop-bought or see
    page 200), a fried egg, drizzle of
    garlic oil (page 202)

Prepare all your ingredients so they're at hand once you start frying, as this is a quick-moving dish. Get your condiments together too, and crack your eggs into a mug ready.

Heat 2 tablespoons of the oil in a wok or large pan set over a high heat. Once the oil is smoking, add the spring onions, garlic and dried shrimps, if using, and stir-fry for 30 seconds. Add the rice, meat/tofu/prawns and vegetables and stir vigorously for 2–3 minutes, squashing any clumpy bits of rice that may remain.

Push everything to one side to create a gap, then slosh in the remaining tablespoon of oil, pour in the eggs, then scramble them in, drawing in the rice. Add the fish and soy sauces, then stir everything well for a minute or 2.

Immediately decant onto plates and add any combination of the suggested garnishes (or none!) as desired and serve immediately.

Ohn htamin

COCONUT RICE

Serves 4

400g long grain or Thai jasmine rice

1 × 400ml tin of coconut milk

2 tsp salt

1 tsp sugar

Crispy fried shallots (shop-bought or
see page 200), to garnish

This is a bit of a treat when you want to add some extra richness
to a meal.

In a sieve, rinse the rice with cold water three times, drain, then
tip the rice into a large, lidded pan, add the coconut milk, salt and
sugar and stir well to combine.

Bring the rice to the boil, then leave to simmer over a low heat
with the lid on for 20 minutes. Halfway through, uncover the pan
and gently fluff the top layer of rice, then replace the lid.

When ready to serve, sprinkle with some fried shallots.

Dhaw but htamin

BUTTER RICE

Serves 4

400g long grain or Thai jasmine rice
2 bay leaves
30g butter, plus a knob at the end
1 tsp white sugar
½ tsp salt

This is an easy way to lift and enrich steamed rice. Slightly fragrant with the addition of bay leaves, you could also add a handful of pre-soaked chana dal to the rice to give a little bit of texture.

In a sieve, rinse the rice with cold water at least three times until the water is running clear. Tip the drained rice into a large lidded saucepan and top with enough fresh water to make the water level double the rice level – about 500ml should do it, but check using your finger to measure the level of water.

Add the remaining ingredients to the pan, then cover and cook over a medium-high heat. Once the water is boiling (more than likely the lid will start bobbing up and down), turn the heat to low. Leave to steam for 10 minutes then check it – the water should all have been absorbed and the grains should be tender. You can leave it to sit on the side, covered, for 10 minutes or so before serving with your desired dishes.

SNACKS

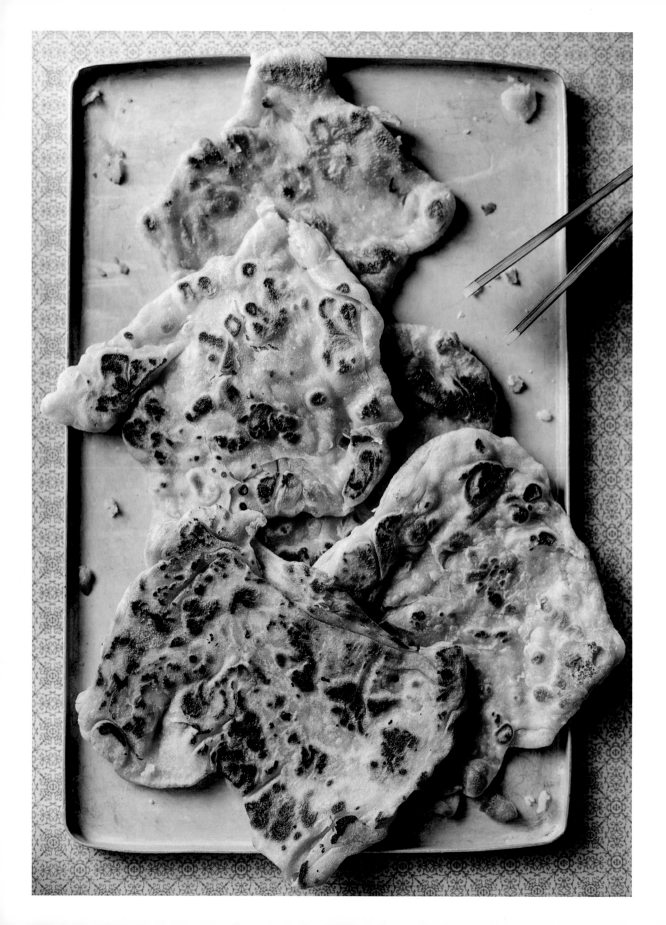

SNACKS

There is a vast range of snacks and street food available all over Burma. One of our many monsoon memories is of a typical day of torrential rain in Yangon, when we ventured downtown to the cinema and outside there was a vendor sat on a stool, hunched over a small bucket of hot oil, frying snacks, barely sheltered by a flimsy compact umbrella. Come rain or shine, there are always snacks!

Many of these snacks involve deep-frying, which isn't always a popular activity, because it can be hot and seems messy. Emily tends to get given this role (Amy: 'but she's just so good at it!'). If you are a little nervous about it, you've got two options: you could get a proper deep-fryer, which are actually very reasonably priced, are very safe and have the advantage of being able to set and control the temperature. Or you could take a deep breath and have a go with a wok. We quite like a wok because the concave shape enables you to get the depth of oil required without having to use a large amount of hot oil on the hob. When frying fritters, such as *paya kyaw* (see page 151), *buthee kyaw* (see page 154) and *kyethun kyaw* (see page 150), you can actually fit quite a lot in a wok without overcrowding. If you do not have a deep-fryer or wok, don't despair, you can still make all of these things in a standard saucepan. What will be invaluable, though, is a suitable heatproof tool with which to retrieve your cooked snacks – a good metal strainer is what you need!

People also wonder what to do with the oil afterwards; with most of these recipes, it will stay neutral so it can be reused to fry again – just strain off any food or scraps of batter first and discard them, then cool and store the oil in a sealed bottle in a cool dark place. You will know when the oil has been reused to its limit and needs discarding – it will look murky or dark and smell bad!

A technique we often use is double-frying, which involves putting everything through an initial fry, resting it (refrigerating if it's going to be some time before you need it), then re-frying briefly just before you want to serve, to crisp up the pieces to perfection. This is handy if you want to prepare lots of pieces in advance.

Lastly, don't worry too much about fried food not being healthy for you. You don't eat it every day, so, like everything in life, do so in moderation and just enjoy it.

Shan Tohu

SHAN (CHICKPEA) TOFU

Makes 1 batch

125g gram/besan (chickpea) flour
½ tsp turmeric powder
½ tsp paprika
200ml cold water
1–2 tbsp oil (vegetable, sunflower or peanut), for greasing
½ tsp salt

Burmese tofu originates from Shan state and, unlike traditional Chinese soy tofu, this is made from gram (chickpea) flour. It is easy to make and is vegan and soy-free. Once set, it is versatile and can be eaten raw in a salad (*tohu thoke*, see page 42) or deep-fried (*tohu kyaw*, see opposite) and served with a tamarind dipping sauce (see page 205). We sometimes double the batch and make it in a 20cm square tin, as it will keep for a few days in the fridge.

Sift the flour into a large bowl (as this affects the smoothness of the finished tofu) with the spices. Whisk in the cold water and leave to sit, uncovered, for 1 hour.

Once the hour has passed, grease a container (a Pyrex dish or baking tin about 10cm × 20cm and at least 4cm deep) with the oil and set aside.

Heat 450ml of water in a large saucepan with the salt. When bubbles are starting to form at the bottom of the pan, gently pour the reserved tofu batter into the pan and start stirring immediately with a wooden spoon, keeping the heat low. Continue stirring, and after a minute or 2 you will notice the batter start to thicken (trust us, you'll know). Stir continuously and cook for at least 5 minutes, to ensure any raw bitter taste does not remain.

Pour the tofu into your prepared greased dish and level off with a knife, then allow to cool at room temperature for at least an hour – you can then refrigerate it to further firm it up. Once firm, cut the tofu into pieces and use in your recipe of choice.

Storage notes
The tofu can be stored in the fridge for 2–3 days, covered. You will need to drain off the excess water prior to using.

Tohu kyaw

FRIED SHAN TOFU

Serves 6–8

1 batch of Shan tofu (see opposite),
 made at least 4 hours earlier
Oil (vegetable, sunflower or peanut),
 for deep-frying
Fine sea salt

This is our favourite thing to make with Shan tofu (see opposite) – it's so incredibly moreish. Delightfully crisp on the outside, with a soft fluffy inside, it's a bit like a good fried chip. We are used to making this in large quantities for supper clubs, so we usually double-fry, by doing the first fry during preparation and a second just before serving.

Decant the block of shan tofu onto some kitchen paper and dab gently to remove the excess water.

Slice the tofu into the desired shape and size – we usually do 2cm × 3cm rectangles, 1cm thick – or you can also cut them into triangles. Either works well.

Pour the oil into a wok or deep saucepan to a depth of at least 5cm and set over a medium-high heat. Line a large plate with a few sheets of kitchen paper.

Test the readiness of the oil with a piece of tofu; it should sizzle at the surface when hot enough (if you have a thermometer it should be 180°C). Add the tofu, frying it in batches – do not overcrowd the pan. It will take about 5 minutes of frying for the tofu to get crispy, turning it occasionally using tongs or chopsticks, to make sure the chunks brown evenly. Scoop out the tofu using a heatproof strainer or sieve and transfer to the plate with kitchen paper.

Season with a sprinkling of salt and serve immediately, ideally with tamarind dipping sauce (see page 205). If you are cooking the tofu in advance, you can set them aside (on top of each other is fine), then just before serving, heat the oil over a high heat and fry for a minute or 2 to crisp up.

Pe kyaw

CRISPY CHANA DAL CRACKERS

Makes about 10 crackers

250g chana dal (or yellow split peas),
    soaked overnight or for at least
    4 hours
75g rice flour
40g plain flour
20g glutinous rice flour (optional,
    replace with 20g rice flour if not
    using)
½ tsp baking powder
½ tsp salt, plus extra to serve
250ml cold water
Oil (vegetable, sunflower or peanut),
    for deep-frying

Storage notes

These can be kept in an airtight container for 3 days. If they aren't as crisp as you'd like you can either deep-fry them again for a couple of minutes or pop them into the oven at 160°C/325°F/gas mark 3 on a baking tray lined with greaseproof paper for 5 minutes for a quick crisp-up.

These are the crunchy delights that make *mohinga* (see pages 88 and 90) truly divine, but you can just have them as a snack on their own. These require a bit of patience to make and the key is not to have the oil too hot when pouring in the batter, so that the characteristic flat cracker shape can form, then turning up the heat to crisp them up. If the oil starts off too hot, the batter will disperse erratically and won't form a stable cracker.

Drain the soaked chana dal in a colander, rinse with cold water and drain again. Empty the dal into a large bowl, along with the flours, baking powder, salt and the cold water and mix well – the batter should have the consistency of whole milk.

Pour the oil into a non-stick frying pan to about 3cm deep and set over a low-medium heat.

Test the readiness of the oil by placing a piece of dal in it; if it gently sizzles without rising to the surface, the oil is ready (if you have a thermometer, it should reach 130–140°C). Turn off the heat.

Stir the batter well with a ladle before scooping up a portion and very gently and slowly pouring it into the pan, keeping the ladle close to the oil's surface. The batter should sink to the base of the pan, making a flat, roundish cracker. You can use the back of the ladle to flatten the dal if it has become a 'mound'. If the pan is big enough, repeat ladling 2–3 crackers in the same way. Set a timer for a minute, then turn the heat back up to high.

Leave the crackers to sizzle gently. They will appear floppy if you prod them, but do not worry – they should slowly rise to the surface and start to turn golden after 5 minutes (encourage them to lift off the bottom of the pan with a fish slice, if needed). Turn them over to cook for another 4–5 minutes. Once nicely golden and crisp, remove carefully and shake off any excess oil. Place on a plate lined with kitchen paper.

Turn off the heat and wait for the oil to cool – this will take about 3 minutes. Repeat the process, making sure you stir the dal batter well before each scoop, turning the heat off for a minute, then turning it back on to high, and so on.

Lightly season the crackers with sea salt and serve.

Kyethun kyaw

ONION FRITTERS
Serves 4–6

2 tbsp gram/besan (chickpea) flour
2 tbsp glutinous rice flour
4 tbsp self-raising flour
1 tsp salt
1 tsp turmeric powder
1 tsp chilli powder
125ml cold water
2 medium onions, peeled and thinly
    sliced
Oil (vegetable, sunflower or peanut),
    for deep-frying

These fritters make a lovely starter and go well with our sour dipping sauce (see page 206). Alternatively, you can use them in *mohinga* (see pages 88 and 90) instead of the *pe kyaw*, or add them to a noodle salad for texture. In order to get the crispiest fritters, try not to overload the onions with batter. *(Recipe pictured overleaf.)*

Place the flours, salt and spices into a mixing bowl. Pour in the cold water and mix with a whisk until you get a smooth, thick batter. Let the mixture rest in the fridge for 1 hour.

When you are ready to cook, pour the oil into a deep pan or wok to a depth of 5cm and set over a medium-high heat. Test whether the oil is hot enough by adding a small amount of batter; if it sizzles and rises to the surface quickly, it is ready.

Pat the onions dry with kitchen paper, then take a small handful and lightly coat them in the batter, shaking off any excess coating – this helps to increase the surface area, producing a much crispier fritter.

Add the fritter to the oil and repeat with 5–6 more fritters, making sure not to overcrowd the pan as this will cool the temperature of the oil. Fry the fritters until they are golden brown. This should take 2–3 minutes.

Scoop out the fritters using a heatproof strainer or sieve and transfer them to a plate lined with kitchen paper to remove the excess oil, then serve immediately while still crisp and hot.

Storage notes
These can be made in advance and fried a second time just before serving. Alternatively, they can also be frozen on the day of cooking for up to 3 months. Defrost carefully, then deep-fry before serving.

Paya kyaw

CHICKPEA FRITTERS
Serves 6–8

Some call these 'Burmese falafel', and you'll see why – they are made from blitzed-up chana dal, with the addition of spices, coriander, garlic and onion, then fried into crispy balls. These are a great street food that can be eaten as they are, or with a dip, or even broken up into a samosa salad (see page 56). These are ideal for preparing in advance then reheating later. *(Recipe pictured overleaf.)*

300g chana dal (or yellow split peas), soaked overnight or for at least 4 hours
Small handful of coriander
2 garlic cloves, peeled
1 medium onion, finely diced by hand (avoid the food processor – it releases too much water)
1 tsp chilli powder
2 tsp paprika
1 tsp turmeric powder
1 tsp fine sea salt, plus extra to serve
Oil (vegetable, sunflower or peanut), for deep-frying

Drain the soaked chana dal in a colander, rinse with cold water and drain again. Set aside a handful of the dal and put the rest in a food processor, along with the coriander (stalks are fine) and garlic. Pulse the contents – you want to keep some texture, but you want it to be processed enough that it holds together. A minute of processing, stopping to push down the pieces that collect up the side, should do it. Empty into a bowl and add the reserved whole chana dal (these will provide a good texture, even if you have over-processed) and the chopped onion, spices and salt. Mix well.

Line a plate with a few sheets of kitchen paper. Pour the oil into a wok or frying pan to a depth of at least 5cm. You can test if it's ready with a piece of chana dal – it will sizzle immediately at the top of the oil. Using your hands, firmly mould walnut-sized balls (or rugby-ball-shapes) of the mixture and gently place in the hot oil. They will turn golden brown and take 3–4 minutes to cook. Scoop out using a heatproof strainer or sieve and transfer to the plate with kitchen paper. Sprinkle with salt, then serve immediately.

Storage notes
These can be kept in an airtight container in the fridge for 3 days. When you want to eat them, either deep-fry them again for a couple of minutes or pop them on a baking tray lined with greaseproof paper and put them into the oven at 160°C/325°F/gas mark 3 for 5 minutes for a quick crisp-up.

Buthee kyaw

GOURD FRITTERS

Serves 4–6 as a snack or starter

This recipe works with other vegetables, such as slices of courgette, sweet potato and aubergine, or florets of broccoli – as tested on Emily's children – so feel free to experiment. Bottle gourd fritters (or indeed marrow, as that's what was easier to get hold of when we were children) would be frequently presented to us at our grandparents' house, usually with a big dollop of tomato ketchup, though you could also serve it with tamarind dipping sauce (see page 205) or sour dipping sauce (see page 206). Here we have two batter recipes because we tried various ones and, actually, both were pretty crispy and delicious. So decide which one you are making based on what you have in your cupboards!

1 medium bottle gourd/dudhi (about 400g) or small marrow, seeds and pith removed

Oil (vegetable, sunflower or peanut), for deep-frying

Fine sea salt

For the rice-flour-based batter

100g rice flour

50g glutinous rice flour

½ tsp bicarbonate of soda

200ml cold water

For the wheat-flour-and-egg-based batter

125g plain flour

1 egg

200ml fridge-cold water

Cut the gourd or marrow into pieces roughly 2cm x 5cm in size, about the thickness of a pound coin.

In a bowl, weigh out the dry ingredients for the batter you are making, then whisk in the liquid components. If making the rice-flour-based batter, whisk until smooth; if making the wheat-flour-and-egg-based batter, just mix until the flour is incorporated but don't worry about lumps.

In a wok or large saucepan, heat enough oil for deep-frying (to a depth of 5cm or so) and line a couple of plates with some kitchen paper. Test the readiness of the oil with a drop of batter; it should sizzle immediately and rise to the surface rapidly.

Dredge the pieces of gourd in the batter, shaking off the excess, and carefully add to the hot oil. They should sizzle and begin to lightly brown as they cook, which should take 4–5 minutes. Fry in batches and do not overcrowd the pan. Remove from the oil, shaking off the excess, and transfer to the plate lined with kitchen paper. Allow to cool, then season with a sprinkling of salt. Serve immediately.

Khauk swe kyut kyut kyaw

CRISPY FRIED NOODLES

Serves 6

This easy treat might revolutionise your choice of beer snack forever. These are also great as a crunchy garnish for dishes like *ohn no khauk swe* (coconut chicken noodles, see page 86). We prefer to use wide rice noodles, such as pad Thai or bun, in this recipe, but you can also use dried egg ones, though they don't bubble up in quite the same way.

Oil (vegetable, sunflower or peanut),
    for deep-frying
200g dried rice or egg noodles

Pour the oil into a wok or deep saucepan to a depth of 5cm and set over a medium-high heat. Line a large bowl with kitchen paper and have a heatproof strainer or sieve ready for fishing out the noodles.

Test the readiness of the oil by popping a piece of noodle into it – it should instantly sizzle (rice noodles will curl up and turn opaque and bubbly). Separate the nest of noodles and add a handful to the oil, frying for a minute, then scoop up with your chosen implement and drain on the kitchen paper. Continue to dry the remaining noodles in batches as above. Try not to finish the bowl yourself before serving.

Storage notes
These will stay crispy in an airtight container for a day or two.

Akyaw zone

CRUNCHY MIX OF BEANS, GARLIC AND NUTS

Makes 1 large jar

This is a component in *lahpet thoke* (pickled tea leaf salad, see page 45) and *gin thoke* (ginger salad, see page 54). It is a mix of crispy delights, including beans, peanuts, garlic and sesame seeds. You can buy this ready-made in Burma or online in the UK. It is actually a pretty good snack on its own, and if you're going to the trouble, you may as well make a decent-sized jar as it will keep well for a couple of months. The ratios of each component aren't strict and can be varied. *(Recipe pictured on page 198.)*

150g sesame seeds

100g raw peanuts, skin-on (ideally)

Oil (vegetable, sunflower or peanut), for deep-frying

100g dried butter beans, soaked in water overnight, then drained and skinned (or use tinned or fresh)

50g chana dal (or yellow split peas), soaked in water overnight or for at least 4 hours (if you don't have these, use more butter beans)

10 garlic cloves, thinly sliced

½ tsp salt

Heat a large frying pan and toast the sesame seeds, stirring occasionally and keeping a close eye on them. Once starting to colour, quickly remove them from the heat and scrape them out into a heatproof bowl to cool. Repeat with the peanuts, stirring occasionally. They will take a bit longer to toast, probably at least 5 minutes, and the skins may start to catch slightly. Test a nut (careful – they'll be hot!) to be sure they don't still taste raw. Once done, transfer to another bowl to cool.

Now it's time to fry. Line two plates with kitchen paper. Heat the oil to a depth of about 5cm in a wok or deep frying pan over a high heat. Test the readiness of the oil by dropping in a piece of butter bean; if it sizzles vigorously and rises to the surface within seconds, it's ready. Add all the beans and deep-fry, stirring and flipping until crunchy and golden – it'll take about 5 minutes. Remove with a slotted spoon and transfer them to the plate lined with kitchen paper.

Using the same hot oil, fry the chana dal; it will take 5–7 minutes for these to become crunchy – test a piece, and if it is still on the chewy side, keep frying. Remove and place on the plate when done.

Finally, fry the garlic slices – keep a close eye on them , they will burn very quickly. Once they're starting to colour, quickly remove them from the oil and lay them on the plate.

Mix the beans, dal, garlic, sesame seeds and peanuts in a big bowl, and add the salt.

Storage notes
Store in an airtight container for up to 1 month.

Buthee hincho

BOTTLE GOURD SOUP

Serves 4–6

This is a simple broth that is traditionally served alongside many Burmese meals. It is almost like an additional beverage, being used to wet the palate and hydrate between mouthfuls of other dishes. We particularly like to serve it with h*tamin let thoke* (rice salad, see page 135), in occasional spoonfuls to add moisture and subtle flavour to the mix. If you wanted to serve the soup as a more substantial dish you could add some glass vermicelli noodles.

1 tbsp dried shrimps
4 garlic cloves
2 tsp salt
⅓ medium-sized bottle gourd
 (about 200g)
Pinch of ground white pepper

Pour 1 litre of water into a large pan. Add all the ingredients, except the gourd and the pepper, and bring to the boil, then turn down the heat and leave to simmer for 10 minutes.

Meanwhile, peel and cut the gourd into batons roughly 1cm wide and 5cm long. Add the gourd to the pan and continue to cook for 15 minutes until soft. Finally, add the pepper before serving.

Storage notes
This soup can be stored in a container in the fridge for up to 4 days.

Seik thar puff

MUTTON PUFFS

Makes 16–18

This is a great way to use up any leftover mutton curry (see page 121). These puffs are often served as a snack at Burmese tea shops, usually accompanied by a cup of milky, sweet tea. If you are up for it, feel free to make your own puff pastry but we think life is too short for that so tend to use shop-bought. Just make sure that you don't use too much of the leftover gravy in the filling otherwise the puffs will come out with a soggy bottom – and nobody wants that.

½ batch of mutton curry (see page 121)
Large handful of coriander leaves, finely chopped (optional)
500g block of puff pastry
Flour, for dusting
1 egg, beaten

Preheat the oven to 180° C/350° F/gas mark 4 and line two baking trays with greaseproof paper.

Scoop out the meat from the curry, carefully shred the meat with a fork and knife and place it in a mixing bowl with the chopped coriander, if using. Add a small amount of the gravy from the curry to the shredded meat, just enough to keep the mixture together.

Roll out the puff pastry on a lightly floured surface to the thickness of a pound coin.

Cut out 16–18 10cm pastry squares. Place a dessertspoon of filling in the middle of each pastry square and brush the edges with the beaten egg. Fold the pastry over the filling to make a rectangle and crimp the edges down with a fork. Make a small cut in the top of the puffs so that any steam can escape, then brush all over the surfaces with more egg.

Place the puffs on the lined baking trays and bake in the oven for 20 minutes until golden brown. Allow to cool for a few minutes before serving.

Storage notes

These can be made in advance and stored in a container in the fridge for up to 4 days, then reheat them in the oven before serving. They can also be frozen on the day of cooking for up to 3 months. Defrost carefully and reheat thoroughly before serving.

Samusa

POTATO AND ONION SAMOSAS

Makes 15

These are commonly found as a street snack or served up in Burmese tea shops with other fried delights. These can also be used in *samusa thoke* (samosa salad, see pages 56 and 58).

There are a few steps to this recipe and the samosa folding takes a bit of practice, but once you've got the knack you will be folding happily and enjoying these crispy triangular delights regularly. They also freeze incredibly well and can be cooked from frozen.

For the filling

1 tsp coriander seeds

1 tsp cumin seeds

1 medium onion, finely chopped

2 garlic cloves, finely chopped

½ thumb-sized piece of ginger, finely chopped

1 green finger chilli, finely chopped

1 tsp garam masala

½ tsp turmeric powder

½ tsp chilli powder

1 tsp salt

300g potatoes, peeled, boiled and roughly mashed

50g frozen peas

Small handful of coriander, roughly chopped

For assembly

2 tbsp plain flour

8 sheets of 25cm square spring roll pastry (we use the Spring Home brand)

Oil (vegetable, sunflower or peanut), for deep-frying

First make the filling. Roughly crush the coriander and cumin seeds using a pestle and mortar.

Heat 2 tablespoons of oil in a frying pan set over a medium heat and add the crushed seeds, frying them until they smell aromatic. Add the onion, garlic, ginger and chilli to the pan and fry for 3–4 minutes until the onions are translucent. Add the rest of the spices and the salt to the pan and stir through for 1 minute.

Place this mixture into a large mixing bowl and add the potato, peas and coriander. Combine well.

To prepare the samosas, make a flour paste by adding 4 tablespoons of water to the flour and stir until you have a thick, glue-like mixture.

Take a pastry sheet and cut it in half diagonally so that you have two triangles. Take one triangle, brush the edges with the flour paste and fold it in half so that you are left with a smaller triangle. Place a finger in the middle of the bottom edge of the triangle while folding the right side over until it hits your finger, then glue down the edge. Bring the left side over the right until you have a pointed cone shape, then glue down the edge.

Open up the cone in your hand and fill with a heaped teaspoon of the samosa filling. Moisten the excess pastry around the edges of the cone and fold one edge inside the cone so that it covers the filling. Bring the last edge over the outside of the samosa so that you are left with a tidy triangle. Repeat with the rest of the pastry until you have 15 samosas.

continued overleaf

When you are ready to fry, pour the oil into a pan to a depth of 5cm and set over a medium-high heat. Test whether the oil is hot enough by adding a small amount of pastry sheet; if it sizzles and rises to the surface, the oil is ready.

Add the samosas to the pan in small batches, as overcrowding can cool the temperature of the oil. Fry the samosas until they are golden brown. This should take 4–5 minutes.

Drain the samosas on kitchen paper to get rid of the excess oil, then serve immediately while still crisp and hot.

Storage notes
These can be made in advance and fried a second time just before serving. Alternatively, they can be frozen on the day of cooking for up to 3 months.

Palata

FLATBREAD
Makes 6 flatbreads

400g plain flour
½ tsp salt
1 tbsp sugar
2 tbsp unsalted butter
225ml cold water
75g unsalted butter, melted
Oil (vegetable, sunflower or peanut),
    for greasing and frying

This is one of our favourite street snacks. We would watch them being effortlessly and expertly thrown across a greased metal table by the vendor until paper thin, then folded and fried. They can be stuffed with sprouted beans, an egg, or simply drizzled with condensed milk. We don't have the secret to the throwing technique (see YouTube for that!), but we do have our own way of stretching the dough, which works for us. This dough needs to rest for 6 hours, so make sure you include this in your planning.

Put the flour, salt, sugar and the 2 tablespoons of butter into a large mixing bowl. Add the water and bring everything together with your hands to form a ball of dough. If it is too dry and there is still excess flour, add a little more water to bring everything together smoothly. Knead the dough by hand for about 5 minutes (or you can use a machine with a dough hook).

Pour 3 tablespoons of the oil onto a large plate. Divide the dough into six equal balls and turn them over in the oil so they're coated in it. Cover the plate with cling film and leave to rest at room temperature for at least 6 hours.

Lightly oil a large area of work surface and take one of your dough balls. Flatten it with the palm of your hand in the centre and stick it to the surface. Taking the nearest edge of the dough, gently lift and pull to stretch it, sticking the edge down on the work surface. Move bit by bit around the circumference, repeating this. It will become thin and translucent, so keep stretching it as you go round. Don't worry if small tears appear, and it doesn't matter if it's an irregular shape. We can usually get one ball to stretch to an area of about 40cm square.

Using a pastry brush, apply a thin layer of the melted butter to the dough. Taking the edge nearest you, fold it over to the centre of the dough. Repeat with the edge that is furthest away, folding it over to meet the folded-over edge. Brush the dough surface with more butter. Take the left edge and fold it a third of the way over, then take the right edge and fold it over that, making a compact square of folded layers of dough. Push down on the dough square with your hands so it's about 20cm square (the dough may have shrunk as you manipulated it).

Heat a tablespoon of oil in a hot, non-stick frying pan and add your dough. Fry on both sides for 2–3 minutes until it starts to crisp and brown. Repeat the process with the rest of the balls.

Kyet thar kyaw

FRIED CHICKEN

Serves 4 as a main with rice;
6 as a snack

'Burmese fried chicken' is one of the most loved street foods. It is seasoned with chilli and turmeric and traditionally served on the bone without a batter. In 2015, Yangon saw the arrival of the first branch of the big international fried chicken joint we all know and love, to huge queues. This is our take on this classic – a hybrid of the old and new, using deboned chicken thighs for speed of cooking and because they are juicier, but you can use breast fillets if you prefer. You could serve this with rice and a dipping sauce (see page 205 or 211) or slice up the chicken to have in *kyet thar thoke* (spiced chicken salad, see page 46).

600g chicken thigh fillets

For the marinade
1 tsp turmeric powder
1 tsp paprika
1 tbsp fish sauce

For the batter
2 eggs, beaten
75g cornflour
75g rice flour
Good grinding of black pepper
½ tsp medium chilli powder (optional, but nice)
½ tsp fine sea salt, plus extra for seasoning
Oil (vegetable, sunflower or peanut), for deep-frying

Cut the chicken into 2cm chunks and mix well with the marinade ingredients in a bowl to coat, then cover with cling film and leave to marinate in the fridge for 1 hour.

When ready to fry, assemble a frying station next to the cooker: one bowl containing the beaten eggs, one containing the mixed flours, black pepper, chilli and ½ tsp sea salt and also a plate lined with kitchen paper ready for the cooked chicken.

Heat the oil to a depth of at least 5cm in a wok or deep saucepan. Test the readiness of the oil with a 1cm piece of bread; if it sizzles vigorously and rises to the surface quickly, the oil is hot enough (it should be about 190°C if you have a thermometer).

Take a piece of chicken and dip it in the egg, then dredge it in the flour mix, ensuring it is covered evenly, and gently place it in the pan to fry for about 5 minutes. Turn the pieces with heatproof tongs to ensure they cook evenly. Check a piece is cooked by cutting it in half, then scoop out the pieces and transfer them to the plate with the kitchen paper and allow to cool slightly. Repeat with the remaining pieces of chicken, but do not overcrowd the pan (you will likely have to do this in 3–4 batches). Season with sea salt and serve.

Cook's notes
These can be made earlier in the day of serving, cooled and stored in the fridge, then deep-fried a second time for a few minutes just before serving. They can also be frozen on the day of cooking for up to 3 months.

SWEETS

အချိုပွဲ

SWEETS

Although people in Burma do like eating sweet things, there isn't a big dessert culture as such. Sweet snacks do have a place throughout the day, or after a main spread of dishes, but they are usually eaten with a cup of tea or coffee rather than taking up a specific course.

Sweet snacks involve coconut, sticky rice, rice flour, tapioca and jaggery, and are often 'accidentally vegan', such as *thargu* (coconut tapioca, see page 187), *kyauk kyaw* (coconut jelly, see page 175), *mont let kauk* (sticky rice doughnuts, see page 192) and *mont let saung* (pandan noodles in coconut milk, see page 182). We love these delights and many are in our repertoire. For our supper clubs, we often make Western desserts that are inspired by the flavours of Burma and that feature mango, lime and coconut. One of our top supper club desserts uses all of these – *thayet thee ohn thee mont* (see page 173), which are light meringues with mango, lime curd and toasted coconut. Our *thayet thee dein gin mont* (mango and lime cheesecake, see page 184) is another winner and was our dad's personal favourite. We would LOVE to use durian more – the intense king of fruits that Mum particularly adores – if only we could source it more easily over here!

When we made our pilgrimage to Dawei, our ancestral hometown, we did some background reading on local foods. We read about a sweet snack called '*ah pone mont*'. Emily mentioned this to Mum as something we ought to check out.

'What's it called?!' she spluttered, choking on her breakfast.

Little did Emily know that it translates to 'vagina cake'! During the rest of our stay we went around the streets, asking people where we could find this elusive dish, which, as you can imagine, we continued to find childishly amusing.

Thayet thee ohn thee mont

MANGO LIME AND COCONUT MERINGUES
Makes 8

This is an absolutely winning combination of flavours that we have served up at several supper clubs over the years. It's perfect for entertaining because the meringues and lime curd can be made the night before, so the dessert only needs a quick assemble just before serving. Our meringue-making method is the Delia Smith one – reliable every time.

For the meringues
3 egg whites
170g caster sugar

For the lime curd
Zest and juice of 2 limes
3 egg yolks
25g unsalted butter
50g caster sugar

For assembly
50g unsweetened desiccated coconut
300ml double cream
200g mango, stoned, peeled and diced into 1cm pieces

Preheat the oven to 150° C/300° F/gas mark 2.

In a clean and dry mixing bowl, whip the egg whites with an electric whisk. Start on a low speed and gradually increase the speed over the next 2–3 minutes to the highest setting until the egg whites are stiff peaks, then stop. Add half the sugar to the egg whites and whisk at high speed, then add the remaining sugar until the meringue is glossy and firm – this usually takes 2 minutes.

Line two baking sheets with greaseproof paper. Spoon four mounds of meringue onto each sheet, spaced out evenly. Using the back of a spoon, make a shallow dip in the centre of each meringue, where the topping will sit once they're cooked. Place the trays in the oven for 35 minutes; once that time is up, switch off the oven and leave the meringues to cool and dry in there overnight.

While the meringues are cooking, prepare the lime curd. Make a bain-marie with a heatproof bowl set over some simmering water (make sure the bowl does not touch the water, though) and add all the ingredients for the curd to the bowl. Stir to dissolve the sugar and melt the butter. Making the curd requires a bit of patience, as it will take anywhere between 6 and 8 minutes to thicken: it should coat the back of a wooden spoon when it is done. We then strain it through a sieve, to get rid of the zest, and let it cool before refrigerating overnight in a covered container.

For the assembly, toast the desiccated coconut in a dry frying pan on the hob, stirring throughout – watch it carefully and don't let it turn brown, it will only take a minute. Whip the double cream until it's thick.

Plate up the meringues, then top each one with a spoonful of cream, a dollop of lime curd, some mango pieces and finally a sprinkling of toasted coconut. Serve immediately.

Storage notes
The meringues can be stored in an airtight container for up to a week. The lime curd can be stored in a sterilised container in the fridge for 1–2 weeks.

Pathein halawa

STICKY RICE SWEETS

Makes 15–20 bite-sized pieces

Pathein is the capital of the Ayeyarwady division, known as the 'rice bowl of Myanmar', which is also famous for the production of this sweet, sticky and buttery snack. It doesn't really count as a dessert, more of a light treat with tea or coffee. It comes in big slabs, that the vendors cut into bite-sized wedges with scissors and sell in pretty containers. Sadly, it doesn't store very well, but chances are it will get polished off pretty quickly, so that won't matter!

2 tbsp oil (vegetable, sunflower or peanut), plus extra for greasing
200g palm sugar or dark brown sugar
100g glutinous rice flour
50g white poppy seeds
100ml good-quality coconut milk
30g unsalted butter, at room temperature

Grease a small brownie tin (or similar-sized container – it can be plastic, porcelain or metal as it won't be heated).

Place 200ml of water and the sugar into a medium saucepan set over a medium heat, stirring occasionally until the sugar has dissolved, and boil gently for 5 minutes until syrupy. Set aside.

Weigh the glutinous rice flour into a heatproof bowl and pour over the syrup, stirring all the time.

Pour this back into your saucepan, along with the poppy seeds, oil, coconut milk and butter. Mix well and return to a low-medium heat, stirring continuously. It should start to thicken and become translucent. After about 5 minutes it should be coming away from the sides of the pan.

Spoon the mixture into your greased container. Allow to cool to room temperature then cut into bite-sized pieces (scissors work best). Eat the same day.

Kyauk kyaw

COCONUT JELLY
Serves 6–8

This refreshing coconut jelly is made with agar-agar, so it's a great option for vegans and non-vegans alike. The beauty of this ingredient is that it sets into a jelly without refrigeration. Use a good-quality coconut milk and the jelly should separate into two layers (top: opaque white; bottom: more translucent), but if it doesn't, it still tastes delicious. We prefer a more gentle texture, which isn't too rigid, hence only needing a small amount of agar-agar.

7g agar-agar strands (or use agar-agar powder, which does not need soaking)
100g caster sugar
½ tsp salt
400ml good-quality (preferably Thai) coconut milk

Cut the agar-agar strands into 2cm lengths with scissors (beware, they will try to escape all over your work surface). Place them in a bowl of cold water and soak for at least 20 minutes, then drain them through a sieve.

Set aside a glass rectangular dish of roughly 15cm × 25cm. Measure 400ml of cold water into a medium saucepan and add the drained agar-agar pieces, caster sugar and salt.

Place the pan on the hob and heat until boiling, stirring regularly to dissolve the sugar and agar-agar. It may take 10 minutes or so for the latter to dissolve fully.

Take the pan off the heat, then pour in the coconut milk and stir until just mixed – do not over-agitate. Pour gently into your prepared dish and leave to set at room temperature (it only takes about an hour but you can speed this up in the fridge).

Once set, cut into diamond shapes. If you have a crinkle-cut knife, even better!

Storage notes
The jelly should keep covered for up to 3 days in the fridge.

Thargu Byin

BAKED COCONUT SAGO
Serves 6–8

In Burma, sweets like this will be prepared in big metal trays then served as square-shaped wedges. It is pretty and delicious – you can use standard white tapioca which will turn colourless on cooking, or the multicoloured type for a bit more vibrancy!

For the bottom layer
Butter, for greasing
200g small tapioca pearls (about 1–2mm diameter)
100g caster sugar
2 tbsp plain flour
3 tbsp coconut cream from a 400ml tin (see Cook's notes), keep the rest for the top layer
½ tsp salt

For the top layer
75g caster sugar, plus 25g for caramelising
75g plain flour
½ tsp salt

Cook's notes
If you can't get hold of tinned coconut cream you can use the 'solid' part of a good-quality coconut milk. Chill two 400ml tins in the fridge for half an hour, then remove them carefully, making sure you don't agitate the tins too much. Open up and scoop out the thick coconut from the top of the tins – you should get at least 400ml. Don't chuck the thinner coconut milk at the bottom, you can use it for making coconut rice, a piña colada or a smoothie.

Grease a 20cm square cake tin or Pyrex dish with butter. Fill a large saucepan with water and heat to boiling point.

Add the tapioca pearls to the boiling water (don't add them too early!) and stir – they should take about 15 minutes to cook and be soft and translucent when done. Stir every few minutes to prevent clumping and sticking to the bottom of the pan (and resulting nightmare washing-up situation). Drain through a sieve set over the sink (the pearls will fall through a colander!) and rinse under the cold tap, stirring to allow as much water to run through as possible, then leave to drain for 5 minutes.

While the tapioca pearls are cooking, get a small pan and add the rest of the ingredients for the bottom layer. Heat gently for a few minutes, just until the sugar has dissolved and it's slightly bubbling. Set aside.

Empty the drained tapioca into a clean bowl, and pour over the bottom layer mix. Stir, and pour into the prepared greased dish. Level with a spoon and pop into the fridge to set for 20 minutes.

Place the top layer ingredients into a clean saucepan, adding the reserved contents of the tin of coconut cream and set over a medium heat. Cook, stirring constantly, for about 5 minutes – it should start to thicken slightly.

Pour this over the set tapioca and level off. Sprinkle the top with the 25g of caster sugar and put the dish under a hot grill for about 5 minutes until light brown spots appear, keeping an eye on it to prevent burning.

Pop the dish back in the fridge to set for an hour, then cut into squares and enjoy.

Ee char kwai

CHINESE DOUGH STICKS

Makes 8–10 sticks

A nod to our dad, who adored these – crunchy, light and bubbly sticks of joy! They originate in China but are eaten all over southeast Asia. We grew up eating these as accompaniments to Dad's steaming bowls of congee (rice porridge), which he made with duck and plenty of spring onions and soy sauce. These sticks can also be cut up with scissors and added to *mohinga* (see pages 88 and 90) to add a crunchy texture. To be honest, we are happiest dipping them into a cup of milky sweet tea ... or a big can of condensed milk!

You can vary the length of your *ee char kwai* depending on the size of pan you have – they need to be completely submerged in the oil to cook properly. *(Recipe pictured on page 170.)*

7g fast-action dried yeast sachet

1 tbsp white sugar

200ml milk

250g plain flour, plus extra for dusting

1 tsp salt

1 tbsp oil (vegetable, sunflower or peanut), plus extra for deep-frying

Dissolve the yeast and sugar in the milk.

Tip the flour into a large mixing bowl, then add the salt, 1 tablespoon of oil and the yeasty milk. Bring it all together with your hands and mix for 5 minutes – you will get a sticky dough. Cover the bowl and leave for 2 hours at room temperature or until doubled in size.

Knock back the dough with your hands and generously flour a clean surface and rolling pin. The dough will be very flexible and stretchy, but do not worry. Roll out into a rectangle of about 20cm × 35cm, the longer side facing you.

Using a sharp knife, slice the dough into rectangles 3cm wide. Taking pairs of alike rectangles, dip a finger in some water and trace the length of one piece then place the other on top and place a skewer or chopstick on top in the midline, along the length of the dough stick, and press down firmly to connect the two pieces.

Heat the oil in a wok or frying pan to a good depth of at least 5cm, set over a high heat. Line a couple of plates with kitchen paper and get a pair of heatproof chopsticks or tongs ready. Test the readiness of the oil by putting a blob of excess dough in it; it should sizzle at the surface instantly when ready.

Pick up a dough stick, holding each end in each of your hands, and gently pull to lengthen the stick, then drop it into the hot oil. Get your chopsticks or tongs and quickly turn the stick around in the oil so it puffs up joyously into that classic stick shape. It will take 2–3 minutes to become lightly brown and gorgeous. Remove from the oil, drain on the kitchen paper and serve.

Storage notes

These will keep for a day in an airtight container and can be crisped up by deep-frying for a couple of minutes, or heated in an oven at 160°C/325°F/gas mark 3 for 10 minutes.

Nham de jar mont

SESAME PRALINE

Makes 1 baking tray

If you've ever been into Sesame Snaps like we were when growing up, this recipe is for you. There would always be a stack of the distinctive yellow packets by the till at the Chinese supermarkets we used to visit with our parents. There are only two ingredients in this recipe, but the important tip is to keep a close eye on the pan when melting the sugar because it can burn very quickly. Also, avoid overstirring the pan or the sugar will start to crystallise. We would suggest serving the praline shards with ice cream or sprinkling the powder over our mango, lime and coconut meringues (see page 173). If you are feeling like a bit of spice you could always try mixing the praline powder with some chilli flakes!

50g sesame seeds
Oil (vegetable, sunflower or peanut), for greasing
200g caster sugar

Toast the sesame seeds in a dry frying pan until they are lightly golden, then set aside. Keep a close eye on them as they can easily burn.

Lightly oil a flat baking sheet and position next to the cooker along with a palette knife (this is so you can spread the praline as quickly as possible).

Sprinkle some of the sugar to coat the base of a thick-bottomed pan and place over a low heat. Once the sugar has started to melt, keep sprinkling the rest of the sugar into the pan bit by bit, gently stirring it with a wooden spoon.

The sugar should caramelise fairly quickly, turning golden brown. At this point add the toasted sesame seeds and stir them into the caramel.

Cook the mixture for another minute, then pour straight onto the prepared baking sheet. Quickly smooth down the praline to as thin a layer as possible with the palette knife, as it will start to solidify within seconds.

Once cool the praline can be roughly broken up into shards or pulsed in a food processor to create a praline powder.

Storage notes
The sesame praline can be stored in an airtight container for up to 1 month.

Sanwin makin

SEMOLINA CAKE

Serves 6–8

We would describe this as *the* cake of Burma – a dense, crumbly, subtly coconut-flavoured cake with a crunchy poppy seed topping. It has probably been the most recipe-tested item in the whole book. We still have the well-annotated recipe of Grandma's to which we have made our own personal adjustments.

100g butter, plus extra for greasing
300g coarse semolina (as coarse as you can find – semolina grits are good)
½ tsp salt
200g palm sugar or brown sugar
50g caster sugar
600ml good-quality coconut milk
4 eggs, beaten
30g white poppy seeds

Grease a 20cm square cake tin with butter and line with greaseproof paper. Preheat the oven to 180° C/350° F/gas mark 4.

Pour the semolina into a large frying pan set over a medium heat. Stir with a wooden spoon occasionally, to toast the grains evenly, for about 5 minutes, then take off the heat and set aside.

Melt the butter, salt and sugars in a large saucepan and stir to dissolve. Add the coconut milk and semolina and stir constantly. The mixture will start to get progressively stiffer and begin to come away from the sides of the pan after about 5 minutes. Take the pan off the heat, add the eggs and stir vigorously to incorporate them and prevent scrambling.

Pour the mix into your prepared baking tin; it doesn't rise so don't worry about leakage if it's pretty full and near the rim of the tin. Level off with a knife and sprinkle the poppy seeds on top.

Bake for 30 minutes; it will feel firm to the touch when done. Allow to cool on a wire rack, cut into diamond shapes and enjoy at room temperature, if you can bear the wait.

Storage notes
Best eaten within 24 hours. You can keep it in the fridge for about 2 days, but it tends to dry out.

Cook's notes
Variations include adding 150g of raisins or a mix of raisins and cashew nuts to the mix. You could also substitute the poppy seeds for sesame seeds, if you prefer.

Mont let saung

PANDAN NOODLES IN SWEET COCONUT MILK

Serves 6

This dessert is very similar to *cendol*, which is found all over southeast Asia. It is very refreshing on a hot day, served with plenty of ice. We would enjoy this after a trip round the hot and sweaty Bogyoke market in Yangon. We call it green worms, which probably sounds a little unappetising but honestly, it's delicious! This can be made in advance, and is better if you do this, as it needs time to chill before serving.

For the coconut milk

½ tsp salt

800ml good-quality (preferably Thai) coconut milk

For the palm sugar syrup

250g palm sugar or dark brown sugar

½ tsp salt

For the pandan noodles

75g fresh pandan leaves, sold in most southeast Asian supermarkets (or you can use 10–15 drops of bottled pandan essence, but it is not quite the same)

50g mung bean flour/starch

50g cornflour

1 tbsp caster sugar

½ tsp salt

First, prepare the coconut milk. Simply stir the salt into the coconut milk in a jug, cover and chill.

Now for the syrup. Take a small saucepan and add the palm sugar (bash it up a bit with a rolling pin if it comes in a large block), 250ml of water and the salt and set it over a medium heat. Stir to dissolve the sugar and salt, then, once boiling, turn down the heat and allow to simmer to a syrupy consistency for about 5 minutes. Allow to cool slightly, then chill in the fridge. Both the coconut milk and syrup need to be cold before serving.

Now make the noodles. Cut the pandan leaves into 10cm strips and place them in a blender with 750ml of water. Blend until the leaves have been completely decimated, with no stalky parts remaining. You should have what appears to be a bright green, rather healthy-looking, soup. Pour the blender contents through a sieve over a jug. You should be left with about 600ml of green pandan extract.

Place the two flours into a clean medium saucepan and add the sugar and salt. Add the pandan water to the pan and stir (note, if using pandan essence, it will be 600ml of cold water and the pandan essence drops).

Place the pan on the hob and heat gently over a low heat, stirring constantly with a wooden spoon. The green mix will begin to thicken very suddenly after a few minutes and start to appear slightly translucent, almost jelly like, and a darker green colour, when this occurs, take the pan off the heat and set aside on a trivet.

Fill a large mixing bowl with cold water and a tray's worth of ice cubes. Get your potato ricer ready if you have one (use the largest 'hole' setting, which should be around 3mm in diameter; alternatively you can use a metal colander with similar-sized holes).

Hold the ricer over the bowl of iced water and spoon 2 heaped tablespoons of pandan mix through the ricer at a time, pushing it through to form short green noodles. Repeat until all the mix is used. Importantly, do not touch or agitate the noodles in the bowl as they need to set, which will take about 20 minutes.

Handle the noodles very gently, removing them from the iced water using a slotted spoon. Place the noodles into glasses (or bowls) then pour over the sugar syrup, layering the coconut milk on top and add a couple of ice cubes (crushed if you like) to each. Present to your guests and remind them to give it a bit of stir before chowing down.

Storage notes
The pandan noodles, coconut milk and syrup can be kept in separate containers in the fridge for about 2 days.

Thayet thee dein gin mont

MANGO AND LIME CHEESECAKE

Serves 6–8

175g ginger nut biscuits

75g butter, melted

500g cream cheese, at room temperature

150ml sour cream

75g caster sugar

3 eggs

Zest and juice of 1 lime

175g mango purée (we tend to use canned Kesar or Alphonso mango purée found in most Asian supermarkets)

Storage notes

This cheesecake can be made the day before and kept in the fridge overnight. It will keep for up to 3 days, but over time the biscuit base will not be as crisp, so it is best eaten on the day of making.

Our dad had a massive sweet tooth and this was definitely one of his favourite desserts. In fact, he would often request a cheesecake instead of a birthday cake.

We would recommend using the bain-marie method in this recipe because it results in a smooth, creamy texture that you just don't get through standard baking. Make sure you wrap the tin well in foil so that it is kept watertight.

Preheat the oven to 180° C/350° F/gas mark 4. Line the bottom of a 20cm springform cake tin with greaseproof paper.

Pulse the ginger nuts in a food processor (or bash with a rolling pin) until you are left with fine crumbs, then mix these thoroughly in a bowl with the melted butter.

Push the biscuit mixture into the base of the cake tin with a spoon or your fingers until even all over, then place in the fridge for at least 20 minutes to firm up.

In a clean bowl, beat the cream cheese with an electric whisk so that it loosens up, then add the sour cream and sugar. Beat in the eggs one by one, then finally add the lime zest and juice and the mango purée.

Take the cake tin out of the fridge and carefully wrap the whole tin in kitchen foil, all over the base and up to the sides so there are no gaps. We would usually do three layers to make sure that the tin is kept watertight. Fill a kettle and bring to the boil.

Pour the mango filling into the cake tin, then place into a high-sided roasting tin. Carefully pour the boiling water into the roasting tin around the cheesecake until it reaches halfway up the side of the cake tin.

Bake in the oven for 1 hour, until the top of the cheesecake has developed a slight skin but keeps a little wobble. Carefully remove the cheesecake from the roasting tin and leave to cool in the tin set on a wire rack.

Once fully cool, place the tin in the fridge. Remove the cheesecake from both the fridge and tin half an hour before serving, to allow it to come up to room temperature.

Shwe yin aye

GOLDEN HEART PUDDING

Serves 8–10

Traditionally, this is served during Thingyan, the Buddhist Burmese New Year festival that occurs around the peak of the dry season. By this point, everyone is yearning for the rains to break and cool everything down, but actually what happens is that during the holiday everyone douses each other with water in one huge water fight. You can even pay to be on a stage with an industrial-sized hose to liberally hydrate passers-by, or you could cool down in a quiet corner with this refreshing dessert. This might seem daunting – with all the different components – but we would suggest making as many of these the day before you want to eat it as they will keep in the fridge, covered.

For the sweet coconut milk
800ml good-quality (preferably Thai) coconut milk
250g caster sugar
1 tsp salt

For the sticky rice
200g glutinous rice, soaked in water overnight

For the tapioca
75g small (1–2mm) tapioca pearls

For assembly
1 batch of coconut jelly, cut into 2cm cubes (see page 175)
1 batch of pandan noodles (see page 182)
3–4 slices of sliced white bread (the cheap kind), each cut into 4 triangles

Storage notes
The components can be stored in the fridge, covered, for up to 2–3 days. You may find they start to dry out a little if left longer than that.

Make the sweet coconut milk by putting the coconut milk, 800ml of water, the sugar and salt into a large pan over the heat. Stir to dissolve the sugar and salt and bring to a simmer, then take off the heat. Allow to cool, then decant into a large jar and chill in the fridge for at least 2 hours.

Meanwhile, drain the soaked sticky rice and place in a bamboo steamer or a heatproof bowl set over a pan of simmering water. Steam for about 15 minutes, then check the grains are soft and pliable, leaving them to cook for longer if they need it. Once done, take the pan off the heat, transfer the rice to a bowl and mix in a tablespoon of the sweet coconut milk (it stops the grains clumping). Set aside to cool.

While the sticky rice steams, cook the tapioca. Fill a medium saucepan with water and bring to the boil, and add the tapioca pearls once it's reached boiling point. Allow to gently simmer, uncovered, for about 15 minutes, stirring occasionally to prevent the tapioca sticking to the bottom of the pan. Once cooked, the tapioca pearls will be soft and translucent. Drain and rinse over a sieve. Pour the drained pearls into a container and stir in a tablespoon of the sweet coconut milk. Leave to cool.

Just before serving, assemble the dessert in bowls: first a dollop of sticky rice, then a dollop of tapioca pearls, followed by 2–3 cubes of coconut jelly and topped with a spoon of pandan noodles. Pour over the chilled sweet coconut milk, add some crushed ice or ice cubes, then top with white bread triangles. Serve immediately.

Thargu

COCONUT TAPIOCA

Serves 6

400ml tin of good-quality coconut milk
400ml cold water
125g caster sugar
1 tsp salt
125g small (1–2mm) tapioca pearls

This is a very simple and light dish of tapioca in sweet coconut milk. It was also one of Dad's favourite desserts, and for his version he would sometimes add little red beans (adzuki beans), which are often used in Asian cooking.

Empty the coconut milk into a saucepan, then fill the tin with the cold water and add that too. Put the pan over a medium heat, add the sugar and salt and stir to dissolve them in the milk, then set aside to cool.

Fill another saucepan with water and heat until boiling, then add the tapioca pearls (the water must be boiling when you add them). Allow to cook for 10–15 minutes until soft and translucent, then stir them around intermittently, as they tend to stick to the bottom.

Once cooked, drain the tapioca through a sieve over the sink with plenty of cold water (to minimise the pearls sticking to each other). Allow to drain. Add the tapioca to the coconut milk and mix well.

This can be eaten hot or cold. If you like, add some ice cubes to make it extra refreshing.

Bein mont

POPPY SEED COCONUT PANCAKE

Makes 4

These sweet, chewy pancakes can be bought from street vendors in Burma as an ideal breakfast on the go. The name literally translates as opium cake, but don't worry, this sugary recipe will give you an altogether different type of high!

For the palm sugar syrup
100g palm sugar

For the batter
100g plain flour
50g rice flour
½ tsp baking powder
125ml coconut milk
1 egg

To cook the pancakes
1 tbsp butter
Handful of fresh or dried coconut flakes
30g white poppy seeds

Make the palm syrup by dissolving the palm sugar in 100ml of water in a pan set over the hob, stirring occasionally. Once boiling, allow it to simmer for a minute or 2 so it slightly thickens but does not become very thick. Set aside to cool for 5 minutes.

Put all the batter ingredients in a bowl and whisk together well with half of the palm sugar syrup.

To cook the pancakes, melt the butter in a non-stick frying pan set over a medium heat, then gently add a ladle of the batter to the pan (or 2–3, depending on the size of your pan). Immediately scatter a few coconut flakes and a pinch of poppy seeds on top of the pancake. Once the top is bubbling and the edges are starting to look cooked, flip over to cook the other side. Repeat until all the batter has been used up.

Drizzle with the remaining syrup and eat!

Faluda

BURMESE FALOODA

Serves 6 generously

For the flan (this will make more flan than you need, but you will enjoy the leftovers)
8 tbsp caster sugar
410g tin of evaporated milk
397g tin of condensed milk
3 eggs
1 tsp vanilla extract

For the rest
1 packet of strawberry jelly
75g small (1–2mm) tapioca pearls
25g basil seeds (optional, but they add a good texture)
Red rose syrup, such as Rooh Afza
1 litre whole milk
6 scoops of vanilla ice cream
Ice (optional)

Falooda originates from the Indian subcontinent and is a milky drink served in a tall glass, often based around a rose sugar syrup, with basil seeds, jellies and ice cream in the mix. Many varieties exist and we don't think you can go too wrong with what you choose to add to it. In Burma, the addition is a delicious lump of custard flan. The drink is served cold, so you will need to allow some time to prepare all the components and chill them.

Preheat the oven to 180° C/350° F/gas mark 4. You need an ovenproof dish of about 20 × 20cm and at least 6cm deep (the shape doesn't matter).

Start with the flan. Melt the sugar in a non-stick pan over a medium heat, watching carefully as it turns to a caramel and shaking the pan gently so that all the sugar melts evenly. Once the sugar is golden brown, pour it into your ovenproof dish, tilting it so the caramel spreads evenly. Set aside to cool.

Next, whisk together the tins of evaporated and condensed milk, eggs and vanilla in a jug and pour over the caramel. Place a sheet of foil over the dish and cook for 1 hour in the oven, until nicely set. Remove from the oven, allow to cool and put in the fridge.

While the flan is in the oven, you can prepare the strawberry jelly – simply follow the packet instructions, pour into a dish and leave it to set in the fridge. Now heat a pan of water on the hob until boiling, then add the tapioca pearls (the water must be boiling when you add them). Allow to cook for 10–15 minutes until soft and translucent, stirring them intermittently as they tend to stick to the bottom. Once cooked, drain the tapioca through a sieve over the sink with plenty of cold water (to minimise the pearls sticking to each other). Allow to drain and set aside.

If you are using basil seeds, simply soak them in cold water and they will plump up into crunchy miniature 'spawn' after 10 minutes.

Once the flan is cool (room temperature will do if your patience is short in supply) and the strawberry jelly is set, you can assemble the falooda in big glasses. Start with 2–3 tablespoons of rose syrup in the bottom of each glass, followed by a dollop of tapioca pearls and soaked basil seeds, if using, a dollop of strawberry jelly, a dollop of flan and a scoop of vanilla ice cream. Pour over the milk, add some ice if you want (if there's space!) and serve, remembering to tell your eager recipients to give the whole thing a stir before diving in.

Mont let kauk

STICKY RICE DOUGHNUTS

Makes about 6

100g glutinous rice flour
40g rice flour
½ tsp baking powder
1 tbsp caster sugar
½ tsp salt
Oil (vegetable, sunflower
    or peanut), for frying
Palm sugar syrup, to serve
    (see page 182)

These chewy, gluten-free doughnuts are served with a sweet syrup, and you will often find these being fried fresh on the streets of Burma, drizzled in palm sugar syrup – you could use the recipe in *mont let saung* (pandan noodles in coconut milk, see page 182).

Weigh out all the dry ingredients and mix them together in a large bowl. Add 200ml of water and mix together with your hands. It will probably be too dry to stick together at this point, so slowly add up to 30ml more water in 5ml increments until you get a smooth dough which isn't too sticky.

Leave the dough to rest in a bowl for an hour. Once the hour is up, line a plate with kitchen paper and fill a wok or saucepan with oil to a depth of at least 5cm, set over a high heat. While the oil is heating up, divide the dough into six pieces.

Test the readiness of the oil with a blob of dough – it's ready if it sizzles rapidly at the surface. (These doughnuts tend to spit when fried so make sure you are wearing long sleeves and an apron – and that there are no children in the vicinity!)

Take a piece of dough and roll it gently between your hands into a sausage about 15cm long. Join the ends together to form a ring and gently place it in the hot oil. They take 2–3 minutes to cook and become crisp but they don't turn a deep brown. Scoop out with a heatproof strainer or sieve and drain on kitchen paper. Serve with palm sugar syrup drizzled on top or in a small dish for dipping on the side.

Dha hnyet mont

PALM SUGAR SPONGE PUDDING WITH COCONUT CARAMEL SAUCE

Serves 8–10

For the sponge
Butter, for greasing
200g pitted dates
250ml boiling water
1 tsp bicarbonate of soda
200g plain flour
2 tsp baking powder
350g palm sugar
2 medium eggs
100g butter, melted

For the coconut caramel sauce
400ml tin of good quality
    coconut milk
½ tsp salt

This is our spin on a sticky toffee pudding, which everyone loves, right? We use palm sugar for the sponge, creating a dark, intense, caramel flavour alongside a divine coconut caramel sauce to pour over. We recommend serving this with a big scoop of ice cream.

Preheat the oven to 180° C/350° F/gas mark 4 and grease a 20cm square baking tin.

Place the dates in a heatproof bowl with the boiling water, then add the bicarbonate of soda. Leave for 5 minutes.

Sift the plain flour and baking powder into a large bowl.

Place 200g of the palm sugar in a food processor to break it down, then add the dates and the soaking liquid and whizz until you have a purée. Mix in the eggs, one by one, followed by the melted butter. Finally add the sifted flour to the date mixture and combine. Pour into the greased baking tray and bake for 30 minutes.

Meanwhile, make the coconut caramel by heating the coconut milk, the remaining 150g of palm sugar and the salt in a heavy-bottomed pan over a medium heat.

Keep stirring until the sugar dissolves, then bring to the boil. Leave to simmer over a low heat and stir occasionally until you have a lightly golden caramel. This should take about 20 minutes.

Check the sponge is cooked by inserting a skewer into the centre – it should come out clean. Pour the caramel over the top of the sponge while it is still in the hot tin. Cut into squares and then serve immediately with ice cream, cream or crème fraîche.

Storage notes
The sponge pudding is best eaten fresh on the day, but it can be kept stored in the fridge for up to 5 days. It should be reheated thoroughly on a low heat in the oven or simply in the microwave.

SAUCES, DIPS AND GARNISHES

အတို့အမြှုပ်

SAUCES, DIPS AND GARNISHES

In this chapter you will find all the essential condiments and garnishes for your Burmese spread. In our kitchens we each have a box containing jars of some of these bits and bobs, ready to assemble into a quick salad when the mood takes us.

In Burma you will find vendors selling salads, very portably, using a host of tubs of different condiments and garnishes on a tray, usually balanced on their heads. This might be as you stroll down any street, travel on the slow-moving train system or relax on the beach. The base ingredient of the salad might be noodles, fritters or a vegetable, which will then be mixed with a variety of components, adding spoons of *hsi jet* (garlic oil, see page 202), *magyi yay* (tamarind water, see page 204), fish sauce, chillies, dried shrimp, lime juice and more. An ingredient that is key to many of these salads, and that you might not have used before, is *pe hmont hlaw* (toasted gram flour, see page 203), which adds a unique, almost nutty, texture.

One of our fondest memories of eating like this was when Mum and Amy decided to catch the Yangon circular train. (This is actually not a very efficient way to get around the city as it is incredibly slow, but it gives you a real flavour of the day-to-day lives of the local people.) As the train progressed through the stations, people came and went, and at one station a large number boarded, carrying large amounts of fresh produce and luggage. Mum overheard their fellow passengers saying,

'What are these stupid tourists doing? They're in the wrong carriage!'

Mum then did what she often does and stopped one of the many food vendors going up and down the train to order a spread of different salads, revealing her fluent Burmese language skills, much to the rest of the carriage's surprise and amusement.

Kyethun hsi /
Kyethun ni kyaw

SHALLOT OIL/ CRISPY FRIED SHALLOTS

Makes 1 large jar

18–20 shallots, peeled
400ml oil (vegetable, sunflower
    or peanut)

This is a delicious oil that can be used in Burmese salads and beyond. Crispy shallots have a fantastic texture and are a taste sensation that can be added to so many things. Although you can use shop-bought fried shallots, homemade taste even better if you have the time and patience to make them.

Cut the shallots in half lengthwise, then slice very thinly into half moons, trying to keep the slices as even as possible (otherwise they won't cook evenly and you will end up with either burnt or soggy bits). Line a plate with a few sheets of kitchen paper.

Heat the oil in a deep, medium saucepan or wok set over a medium-high heat. Do not leave the pan unattended. Have a heatproof strainer or sieve ready for fishing out the shallots. Test the readiness of the oil by placing a piece of shallot in it; if it sizzles and comes to the surface within a few seconds, the oil is ready.

Add a large handful of shallots to the hot oil. Keep a close eye on it and carefully stir the pieces regularly, being careful not to splash the hot oil on yourself. Turn the heat down if they are colouring quickly – we sometimes remove the pan from the heat completely for a minute or so if it's doing this. Shallots take longer to crisp up than garlic, requiring probably a few minutes of frying. Also you'll need to do this in batches – trust us.

Once the shallots are golden and crisp, scoop them out quickly from the oil using a heatproof strainer or sieve and transfer to the plate with the kitchen paper. Continue frying the shallots in handful-sized batches until all are cooked, then transfer to the kitchen paper, as before. It doesn't matter if a few pieces remain in the oil at the end.

Allow the oil to cool, then pour into a clean, sealable jar; store the crispy shallots in an airtight container to use as a garnish in lots of recipes.

Storage notes
Shallot oil can be stored in a cool, dark place for up to 1 month. Separate crispy shallots can be kept in an airtight container in a cool place for about a week (after this they tend to lose their crispness).

Hsi jet /
Kyethun phyu kyaw

GARLIC OIL/
CRISPY GARLIC

Makes 1 large jar

There is always a jar of garlic oil in our kitchens. It features in most of the salads that we make, but it is also used as a condiment in several noodle dishes, such as *shan khauk swe* (Shan noodles, see page 94) or *hsi jet khauk swe* (garlic oil noodles, see page 96). To be perfectly honest, there are probably loads of dishes, Burmese or otherwise, that could be optimised with a drizzle of this garlicky nectar, especially with its crispy garlic pieces that create little flavour bombs on your palate. We don't cut the garlic pieces too small as they tend to burn quickly when cooking, but if you prefer smaller pieces, then chop away!

3 bulbs of garlic, peeled
400ml oil (vegetable, sunflower or peanut)
1 tsp turmeric powder

Separate the garlic cloves and slice them as thinly and evenly as you can. Make yourself comfortable, maybe sit yourself in front of some mindless television, as it will take time. It can also make your fingers feel a bit burny, so you might want to put on disposable gloves for this. Line a plate with a few sheets of kitchen paper.

Heat the oil in a deep, medium saucepan or wok set over a medium-high heat. Do not leave the pan unattended. Have a heatproof strainer or sieve ready for fishing out the garlic pieces. Test the readiness of the oil by placing a piece of garlic in it; if it sizzles and comes to the surface within a few seconds, the oil is ready and you can add all the garlic at once, turning the heat down to low.

Keep a close eye on the garlic, turning the pieces regularly in the oil, being careful not to splash hot oil on yourself. Turn the heat down if the garlic is colouring quickly – we sometimes remove the pan from the heat completely for a minute or so if it's doing this. Once the garlic pieces are golden brown and crisp, take the pan off the heat.

Scoop out the crispy garlic pieces using a heatproof strainer or sieve and transfer them to the plate with the kitchen paper, to stop them cooking further. It doesn't matter if a few pieces remain in the oil.

Stir the turmeric into the oil and leave to cool. Once cool, pour the garlic oil into a clean, sealable bottle. You can then return the reserved crispy garlic pieces to the oil (they will remain crispy) or keep them separate to garnish other dishes or combine into *balachaung* (see page 212).

Storage notes

The oil can be stored in an airtight bottle in a cool, dark place for up to 1 month, though in our house there's rarely any left by that point! If you are keeping the crispy garlic pieces separate, they can be stored in an airtight container in a cool place for 2–3 weeks.

Pe hmont hlaw

TOASTED GRAM FLOUR

This is a key part of our '*a thoke*' (salad) station, it adds a slightly nutty flavour and helps to bind the components in a way that we find difficult to describe, but if it's missing, you just KNOW. We also use it to thicken *ohn no khauk swe* (coconut chicken noodles, see page 86).

Gram/besan (chickpea) flour – 200g is a good amount for about 2 salads, but you can make as much or as little as you like

Sift the gram flour into a bowl, as it is usually quite lumpy. Heat a clean dry frying pan over a low-medium heat and add the flour. Stir around so it is distributed evenly and continue to stir intermittently, to ensure even toasting. It will begin to smell slightly nutty and will brown slightly after about 5 minutes. It may clump a little, which is normal; you can always re-sift it if it is particularly clumpy.

Tip into a bowl and allow to cool before storing in an airtight container. It should keep well for 3 months.

Magyi yay

TAMARIND WATER

Makes 1 batch

25g tamarind pulp
100ml hot water

This is used throughout the books in recipes such as *tohu thoke* (Shan tofu salad, see page 42), *kyet u hin* (egg curry, see page 107) and *magyi wet thar hin* (pork tamarind curry, see page 123).

If you can't get hold of tamarind pulp, you can substitute it with a teaspoon of ready-made tamarind paste mixed with 100ml of hot water.

Put the tamarind pulp into a heatproof bowl, pour the hot water over and allow to steep for 5 minutes.

Using your hands, squeeze the pulp, separating the flesh from the seeds and allowing the tamarind to disperse. Leave to steep for a further 5 minutes, then to separate the seeds from the water, pour the contents into a sieve placed over another clean bowl.

Storage notes
The tamarind water could be stored in a fridge, covered, for use in recipes for up to a week.

Magyi achin yay

TAMARIND DIPPING SAUCE

Makes 1 small bowl

A spicy-sour dip that goes perfectly with the *tohu kyaw* (fried Shan tofu, see page 147) or *paya kyaw* (chickpea fritters, see page 151) – we have served this on many occasions at our supper clubs and it is especially delicious with the fritters.

2 batches of tamarind water, freshly
    made (see opposite)
½ tsp sugar
½ tsp salt
1 garlic clove, peeled
½ bird's eye red chilli, roughly chopped

Make a double batch of tamarind water (see opposite) and while it is still warm, add the sugar and salt and stir until they dissolve.

Pound the garlic and red chilli using a pestle and mortar to form a paste. Add them to the tamarind water, stirring well to combine.

Storage notes
This sauce is best made and served fresh on the day.

Achin yay

SOUR DIPPING SAUCE

Makes 1 small bowl

This dipping sauce packs a punch and goes particularly well with *kyethun kyaw* (onion fritters, see page 150). It can be served alongside any of our fried snacks to cut through the oil.

If you can't get hold of tamarind pulp, you can substitute it with a teaspoon of ready-made tamarind paste mixed with 100ml of hot water.

50ml boiling water
25g tamarind pulp
1 tbsp palm sugar
2 garlic cloves, peeled
½ thumb-sized piece of ginger, peeled
1 bird's eye red chilli
1 tsp fish sauce

Prepare the tamarind by adding 50ml of boiling water to the tamarind pulp in a heatproof bowl and leave for a few minutes. Use a fork to further break up the pulp, then strain through a sieve, discarding any stones, so you are left with the tamarind water.

While the tamarind water is still warm, add the palm sugar and mix until it dissolves.

Crush the garlic, ginger and chilli to a paste using a pestle and mortar or blitz in a food processor. Add the paste and the fish sauce to the tamarind, mix well and serve.

Storage notes
This sauce is best made and served fresh on the day.

Amay nga yok chin

MUM'S DIPPING SAUCE

Makes 1 small bowl

This is something that Mum would often whip up to serve alongside rice and curry. You just need to add a small amount to your spoon in between mouthfuls of curry to create another layer of depth and flavour, especially if you like things spicy.

2 garlic cloves, finely chopped
1 bird's eye red chilli, finely chopped
Juice of ½ lime
2 tbsp fish sauce
2 tsp palm sugar

Place the garlic and red chilli to a small bowl, then tip in the rest of the ingredients, mix well and serve.

Storage notes
This sauce is best made and served fresh on the day.

Thit thee a myo myo

MIXED VEGETABLE PLATTER

Serves 4–6

As part of most Burmese dinner spreads you will find a platter of raw and blanched vegetables surrounding a bowl of funky shrimp- or fish-based savoury dip. You could set up a platter of vegetables to serve with any of the dipping sauces in this section, we've suggested some vegetables here but feel free to vary the selection depending on what you have in your fridge. (*Recipe pictured overleaf.*)

1 handful green beans, blanched
½ cucumber, cut into batons
2 medium carrots, peeled and cut into batons
1 pepper, cut into batons
1 handful radishes

Prepare the vegetables and arrange on a large plate with your chosen dipping sauce (or sauces) in the centre. Serve alongside other dishes.

Nga yote thee hsi

CHILLI OIL
Makes 1 small jar

There is always a jar of chilli oil on the table at home for adding some extra spice to curries, fried rice and literally any dish. For dishes that have additional chilli flakes on the side, such as *ohn no khauk swe* (coconut chicken noodles, see page 86) or *mohinga* (see pages 88 and 90), you could use this instead.

250ml oil (vegetable, sunflower or peanut)
5 garlic cloves, peeled
1 tbsp dried shrimps
6 tbsp chilli flakes
1 tsp fish sauce

Heat the oil in a frying pan set over a low heat.

Crush the garlic to a paste using a pestle and mortar or blitz in a food processor.

Slowly fry the minced garlic in the oil for 10 minutes – it should slowly turn golden brown and gently infuse the oil.

Meanwhile, pound the dried shrimps using a pestle and mortar or use a food processor to create a powder. Place the powder in a heatproof bowl with the chilli flakes and fish sauce.

When the garlic is golden brown, carefully pour the garlic and oil over the shrimp, chilli and fish sauce mixture and stir thoroughly.

Leave the chilli oil to come to room temperature before transferring it to a clean airtight bottle.

Storage notes
The chilli oil should ideally be left for a couple of days to fully infuse before using. Once opened, it can be stored in an airtight jar in the fridge for up to 2 months.

Ngapi chet

TOMATO AND SHRIMP SAUCE

Serves 4 as a side

This sauce has a number of different uses; it can be eaten alongside rice and curries or used as a dip with the vegetable platter (see page 207). We have also tried it with spaghetti as a Burmese 'bolognese' – delicious! It is best served at room temperature.

9 tbsp oil (vegetable, sunflower or peanut)
1 medium onion, finely chopped
6 garlic cloves, finely chopped
2 tsp dried shrimps
1 tsp shrimp paste
1 tsp chilli powder
2 tsp fish sauce
1 × 400g tin of chopped tomatoes

Heat the oil in a frying pan set over a medium heat. Add the onion and garlic and fry for a few minutes until soft.

Meanwhile, pound the dried shrimps to a powder using a pestle and mortar or food processor.

Dissolve the shrimp paste and shrimp powder into the onion and garlic mixture over the heat, then add the rest of the ingredients. Simmer for 10 minutes until the sauce has thickened, then take off the heat and leave to cool.

Storage notes
Can be stored in a container in the fridge for up to 4 days or frozen on the day of cooking for up to 3 months. Defrost carefully and reheat thoroughly before serving.

Balachaung

CRISPY SHRIMP SHALLOT RELISH

Makes 1 × 500ml jar

100g dried shrimps

Oil (vegetable, sunflower or peanut),
for deep-frying

2 bulbs of garlic, finely sliced

10 shallots, peeled and finely sliced

2 tbsp chilli flakes (or more to taste)

1 tsp sugar

1 tsp salt

This is an incredible dry relish made up of crispy fried garlic, shallots and shrimp but with a spicy kick. It can be served simply with rice or among a big spread of curries and salads, but it has also been known to end up in a sandwich (ideally a cheap, white, sliced loaf slathered with butter) or spooned directly into one's mouth from the jar. You need to keep a close eye on the pan when frying the components, as they can burn quickly. It does take a bit of effort and patience and will result in a pungent-smelling kitchen, but it is so worth it and you can always make up a big batch to be kept for future use.

Pound the dried shrimps using a pestle and mortar or use a food processor to create a shrimp powder. Open the windows and turn on the extractor fan.

Line a few plates with some sheets of kitchen paper. Pour the oil into a deep saucepan or wok to at least a depth of 5cm and set over a medium heat. Test the readiness of the oil by placing a piece of garlic in it; if it sizzles and comes to the surface within a few seconds, the oil is ready.

Add all the garlic and fry until crisp and golden brown. This should only take a couple of minutes, but you need to watch closely because it can burn rapidly. Remove the garlic pieces from the oil using a heatproof strainer or sieve and transfer to the kitchen paper.

Fry the shallots in the same pan of oil, in batches, until crisp and golden brown, then remove to cool and dry by placing on a fresh piece of kitchen paper. This may take 3–5 minutes per batch, but again, watch closely!

Finally, add the shrimp powder to the same pan. It will sizzle and foam and you will probably be concerned, but don't worry, it is normal! Keep stirring for 2–3 minutes, then scoop out again and leave to dry on a fresh piece of kitchen paper. The shrimp powder becomes crispy on cooling.

Once the fried garlic, shallots and shrimp are cool, combine them in a mixing bowl, then add the chilli, sugar and salt and mix well.

Storage notes
Once made it can be kept in an airtight jar for up to 1 month; it may slightly lose its crispiness over time but it will still be delicious.

STOCKISTS AND SUPPLIERS

There have been great advances in the range of goods available in the major supermarkets over the years, and it is standard now for them to have a dedicated world foods aisle, which we find fascinating. It usually features products for Chinese, Japanese and Indian cooking – and beyond. Some supermarkets even have an Asian section for fresh produce (talking about you, Asda Leyton Mills). We are lucky to live in East London, which has a diverse demographic and so is heaving with independent grocers with a constant supply of fresh coriander, limes and our favourite large, orange-netted sacks of onions.

There are still a few specialist items for which you will need to visit an Asian supermarket. Alternatively, there are lots of online stores which are increasingly well stocked.

We have compiled a list here of some of our trusted suppliers.

THE LOST TEA COMPANY

www.lostteacompany.com

The Lost Tea Company brings tea in both drinking and fermented form from the hills of Shan State to the UK. You can buy both tea and crunchy bean mix online and at a few retailers listed on their website.

LONGDAN (Vietnamese supermarket)

www.longdan.co.uk

A number of branches – Leyton Cash & Carry, Shoreditch, Kingston upon Thames, Elephant & Castle, Hoxton, Camden Town

This Vietnamese supermarket chain sells a variety of east Asian products, including fresh produce. We tend to buy most of our fresh ingredients, such as green mango, papaya and pandan leaves, from here. They are also stockists of elusive basil seeds! They have a large frozen foods section, which is great for buying big packets of good-quality prawns and lime leaves.

LOON FUNG (Chinese supermarket)

www.loonfung.com

A number of branches – Chinatown, Stratford, Tottenham, Colindale, Alperton

Excellent range of east and southeast Asian products. Some branches have a butcher and fresh seafood counter.

MUM'S HOUSE (Burmese supermarket)

www.mumhouse.com

This Burmese online supermarket offers a delivery service. It sells a wide range of products, including lahpet, Mum's favourite preserved sour fruits, spices and their own *balachaung*, alongside other Burmese paraphernalia. You can also order cooked food in advance, though we haven't tried this.

TAJ STORES (South Asian supermarket)

112 Brick Lane, Spitalfields, London E1 6RL

This is a long-established supermarket selling a large selection of products from the Indian subcontinent, including fresh goods and it also has a butcher's section.

WING YIP (Chinese supermarket)

www.wingyip.com

A number of branches – Birmingham, Manchester, Croydon, Cricklewood

This large, often cavernous, Chinese supermarket chain is great for buying a wide range of Asian products. Some of them have their own butcher and fishmonger on site. We have many memories of enjoying a dim sum feast at the Croydon branch, pre or post stocking up on shopping next door.

SOUSCHEF

www.souschef.co.uk

This online company sells a range of different products from all over the world, but it does have a particularly good Asian section, with more specialist items on offer, such as basil seeds, noodles and sauces.

WAI YEE HONG

www.waiyeehong.com

Eastgate Oriental City, Eastgate Road, Eastville, Bristol, BS5 6XX

A Chinese cash and carry and supermarket that stocks an excellent range of products from east and southeast Asia. They also offer delivery, beyond their local area, with very reasonable delivery charges.

ACKNOWLEDGEMENTS

When we started the supper club, we had no idea that we would end up here, writing our own cookbook. Every year at Christmas, at least one cookbook would be exchanged between us as a present, which we would browse in between peeling potatoes and criss-crossing Brussels sprouts. It still seems unreal that we will now have our own.

Firstly we want to thank our Mum for teaching us pretty much everything we know about Burmese cookery, encouraging and supporting us in all our ventures, working hard and sacrificing so much of yourself to give us the lives that we have. We are so lucky to have you. We search for your approval in everything we do, so we hope this book passes the test. Thank you Dad for instilling the importance of knowing your roots, your sense of humour, your excellent cabbage slicing skills. As much as we would get annoyed by your ways, you would do anything for us and we know you were proud of what we had achieved. We miss the random vegetables/possibly useful items you'd bring over when you visited. We can imagine you telling all your friends (and probably lots of strangers too) about this book and we wish you could be here to see it complete. Thank you to Grandma Ruby for looking after us when we were little, your recipes and delicious cooking, and for being a fierce matriarch and role model to us.

Big thanks to our long-suffering husbands, Ned and Matthew. They work hard enough as 'proper' doctors so when they help out with childcare, the wine list or KP after doing a night shift, we are tremendously grateful. You never complain when we host events, you are patient and tolerant and put up with our to-do-lists. Thank you to Emily's children, Grace and Wilf, for being cute and providing us with cuddles and laughs. Hopefully you'll love cooking too and can cook some of these recipes for us one day.

Thinking back to where we started, we have to thank Will Wong. Without you saying yes to us at our first supper club who knows what might have happened! We are forever grateful to you for giving us that chance and starting the ball rolling. Then the inspirational Asma Khan, for getting us back into it after the first baby hiatus; Danny and Steve at Tina We Salute You E20, for trusting us to take over your whole venue on a Saturday night. We are also so grateful to our wonderful helpers and friends – Ameeta, David, Liz and Sean. You truly know who your friends are when they volunteer without question to work a hard 12 hour shift, clearing plates, serving guests and doing endless laborious chopping tasks, all with a smile. You are amazing.

Another thank you goes to our 'other sister', MiMi Aye – our friend and go-to knowledge base for all things Burmese. Thank you for all your help and the laughs over the years.

Throughout the past few years we have gained support from people we have respected for a long time within the food world. Grace Dent, without a doubt you have been our champion, opening doors to much more than we would have ever expected. You are always welcome at our table. And much gratitude to *Observer Food Monthly* for that unexpected share of the cover with Jeremy Corbyn and Moby.

With the creation of this book we have been guided by a great crew of people who we want to thank. Victoria Hobbs, our agent, we loved you from the start, trekking to the darkest depths of East London through treacherous snow just to meet with us. We were yours. Louise McKeever, your enthusiasm started this book going, and Celia Palazzo seamlessly picked it up and completed the journey with us. Thank you to Clare Skeats who came up with the great design which is so very us. Martin Poole, our photographer, we are so thankful for your dedication and perfectionism that has led to these beautiful photos (plus, the gossip and laughs). Thanks to Jo Harris for choosing props we loved! And last but not least, Aya Nishimura, food stylist of dreams – you are so calm, so thoughtful in your work. We could not have asked for a better shoot team and we had such a lovely time with you all.

Finally, thank you to everyone we have cooked for at our supper clubs, particularly our repeat attenders. You've kept us going and hope you'll keep doing so even though you can now recreate the food at home yourselves!

INDEX

Recipe photographs separated from their recipes are in **bold**

10 9 8 7 6 5 4 3 2 1

Ebury Press, an imprint of Ebury Publishing,
20 Vauxhall Bridge Road,
London, SW1V 2SA

Ebury Press is part of the Penguin Random House group
of companies whose addresses can be found at
global.penguinrandomhouse.com

Penguin
Random House
UK

First published by Ebury Press in 2020
www.penguin.co.uk

A CIP catalogue record for this book is available from
the British Library

Publishing Director: Lizzy Gray
Project Editor: Celia Palazzo
Design: Clare Skeats
Cover and chapter opener design: Two Associates
Photography: Martin Poole
Food styling: Aya Nishimura
Prop styling: Jo Harris
Production: Serena Nazareth

ISBN: 978-1-52910-320-5

Colour origination by Altaimage Ltd, London
Printed and bound in China by C&C Offset Printing Co., Ltd

Penguin Random House is committed to a sustainable future
for our business, our readers and our planet. This book is made
from Forest Stewardship Council® certified paper.